C0-DUN-848

A Catholic

Response

to the Asian

Presence

©1990, National Catholic Educational Association
1077 30th Street, N.W., Suite 100
Washington, D.C. 20007-3852

ISBN No.1 55833 057-7

Table of Contents

We believe in One God

Tôi tin kính môt Thiên Chúa

Vietnamese

ຂ້າພະເຈົ້າ ເຊື່ອ ເຖິງ
ພຣະະເປັນເຈົ້າ

Laotian

Kuv ntseeg txog Huab Tais Ntuj

Hmong

전능하신 천주 성부

Korean

ខ្ញុំជឿ ព្រះបិតា

Cambodian

我（我們）信 唯 一 的 主。

Chinese

われは、天地の創造主、全能の父なる天主を信じ、

Japanese

**SUMASAMPALATAYA
AKO SA ISANG DIYOS**

Philippine

ഏകദൈവത്തിൽ ഞാൻ വിശ്വസിക്കുന്നു.

Indian

Acknowledgements

A *Catholic Response to the Asian Presence* is the product of a collaborative effort of a number of Asian parents, educators and ministers, and also of many non-Asian Church leaders who minister with the various Asian communities within the United States.

Special thanks are due to the Asian parents who took the time to attend the national hearings sponsored by NCEA's Special Educational Service Department, USCC's Office of Migration and Refugee Services, and the Archdiocese of New York's Office of Pastoral Research and Planning.

Gratitude is also due to the many lay ministers, sisters and clergy of the dioceses in which the hearings were held—Baltimore, Boston, Chicago, Honolulu, Los Angeles, New York, Oakland, Philadelphia, Portland, San Francisco, Seattle, St. Paul/Minneapolis. They participated with energy and commitment in searching together for ways to respond effectively to the Asian presence in this country.

We are especially indebted to the diocesan contact persons who organized all facets of the hearings—invitations, space, prayer, and meals. They selected a rich mix of parents, educators and ministers to reflect on the Church's mission with Asian peoples within their respective dioceses; they then assured a productive time together by their able administration of all the details.

For the gift of their time and commitment we thank the following diocesan contact persons: Baltimore, Sr. Rosalie Murphy; Boston, Fr. William Schmidt; Chicago, Fr. William O'Brien; Honolulu, Ms. Cecile Motus; Los Angeles, Sr. Lucia Tu; New York, Mrs. Ruth Doyle; Oakland, Fr. George Crespin; Philadelphia, Mr. Thomas Forkin and Sr. Mary Louis Sullivan; Portland, Fr. Vincent Minh; San Francisco, Bishop Carlos Sevilla; Seattle, Ms. Veronica Barber and Ms. Esther Lucero; and St. Paul/Minneapolis, Mr. Thomas Kosel.

There were many members of various Asian communities who provided us with information and resources; we are grateful to them for enriching this publication.

And finally, thanks to Mrs. D.J. Rivenberg who helped with the copy editing, and to Mrs. Geri Garvey and Mrs. Tia Gray of the NCEA staff who assisted most ably in getting this publication into print.

Funding for the development of this manuscript came from the following groups: the Fr. Michael McGivney Fund for New Initiatives in Catholic Education which is sponsored by the Knights of Columbus; the Maryknoll Fathers; the National Catholic Educational Association and an anonymous foundation. We are grateful to all of these organizations for their support of this project. In addition, we are grateful to Mr. Peter Robinson who assisted the authors and editors in securing funding from various other sources.

Contributing
Authors

Maria de la Cruz Aymes, SH

Sister Maria de la Cruz is the author of religion textbooks for Catholic schools and parish religious education centers. She teaches seminarians from a variety of ethnic communities at St. Patrick's seminary, Menlo Park, California.

Noemi M. Castillo

Ms. Castillo was born, raised, and educated in the Philippines, and migrated to the United States on December 25, 1974. She is the Director of the Office of Filipino Catholic Affairs, Archdiocese of San Francisco, California.

Ruth Narita Doyle

Mrs. Doyle is the Director of the Office of Pastoral Research and Planning, Archdiocese of New York, New York. She was the principal researcher on studies of the Hispanic and Black communities in the Archdiocese of New York and has conducted extensive research on parish life and ethnic groups.

Thomas M. Gannon, SJ

Fr. Gannon is a member of the Jesuit Provincial Staff, Chicago, Illinois, and has been a visiting professor of sociology and theology in India, Japan, Austria, Germany and England. Also, he edited *World Catholicism in Transition*.

Suzanne E. Hall, SNDdeN

Sister Suzanne is the Executive Director of the Special Educational Services Department, NCEA, Washington, D.C. She has written and edited reports and publications on ethnic communities within the Church and, also, on the Church's responsibilities to marginalized persons and communities—the handicapped, the poor, and new immigrants.

Cecilia Li

Mrs. Li is an educational consultant, and the director of two Day Care centers sponsored by the Chinese American Planning Council for New York, New York. Currently, she is president of the Greater Chinatown Community Association and a member of the 18th Synod of the Archdiocese of New York.

Iwao Peter Munakata

Dr. Munakata is Professor of Sociology at Sophia University, Tokyo, Japan. His doctorate is from Fordham University, and he is a member of the Pontifical Council for Non-Believers.

Peter Tran, CSsR

Fr. Tran is Special Assistant to the Director of the Office for Pastoral Care of Migrants and Refugees, Migration and Refugee Service, United States Catholic Conference, Washington, D.C.

EDITORS
Suzanne E. Hall, SNDdeN
Ruth Narita Doyle
Peter Tran, CSsR

Introduction

Our country has always been singularly blessed with the presence of people from many cultures. Our newest immigrants from Asian countries bring with them a richness of traditions from background very different from most of us. It is important that we understand and be sensitive to their needs. It is crucial that we support and enable their understanding and loyalty to their faith to come out of the traditions which they value strongly.

For the Church as we look to the next century, the inculturation of faith is a major challenge and one in which we must strive to be open to new directions. This response to the Asian communities is an important beginning for all of us to try to truly grasp the meaning of the universality of our faith.

John Cardinal O'Connor
Archbishop of New York

The possibility of Asian migration to the United States has taken a decidedly different turn from the first exclusionary law against Asians in the Chinese Exclusion Act of 1882. During the last decade, Asians have accounted for more than half of both the immigrant and refugee movements to the United States. In concrete terms, Asians will number at least 8 million, as the demographic complexion of the U.S. changes in the 1990s. Our country has made it possible for Asians to come to the U.S. Now, it remains for the Church to make these newcomers welcome.

The ministry of welcome is exercised by the Church in three basic activities. The pastoral care of Catholic Asian migrants is a duty incumbent on the local Church as outlined in Church law and documents. The evangelization of the non-Christian Asian newcomers is an opportunity which the Church cannot neglect. The provision of migration, resettlement, educational and other services is a concrete manifestation of the ministry of welcome the Church can exercise.

In 1986, the National Conference of Catholic Bishops issued a statement entitled "Together a New People." This pastoral statement on migrants and refugees gives encouragement and commitment to the ministry of welcome I have described. The study contained in this book is largely a response to the challenge issued by this pastoral statement. But as one takes up one challenge, many more become evident.

The collaborative effort which produced this important study is a model for an integrated approach to welcoming the Asian newcomer to our land and to our Church. I recommend it to you for reading and implementation.

Rev. Msgr. Nicholas DiMarzio
Executive Director
Migration and Refugee Services
United States Catholic Conference

T his publication grew out of a series of hearings sponsored by the National Catholic Educational Association, the Office of Pastoral Research and Planning, Archdiocese of New York, and Migration and Refugee Services, United States Catholic Conference. We believe that the positions set forth in this volume are a faithful reflection of the views expressed by the representatives of a wide variety of Asian American groups. They are also a challenge to us to develop new attitudes and approaches, new materials and methodologies in our Catholic schools and catechetical programs that seek to serve our expanding Asian population.

In a number of the hearings, parents stated very clear expectations of Catholic schools—education in faith, discipline, moral training, counter-cultural value system, and security—this along with a *very* strong academic program. At the same time, Asian parents want their children to retain some of their native culture and traditions, and hope that the Church here will assist them in accomplishing this goal.

In regard to religious education, the respondents noted further needs for opportunities to learn more about the contemporary teachings of the Church, about parenting skills, and about ways of maintaining traditional values in our "materialistic" society. There was also an interest in religious education for non-Catholics (many of them non-Christians), especially on the part of those parents who are the products of Catholic education in their homelands.

In addition, the respondents at the hearings offered many general recommendations which should be heeded by both school personnel and catechists. Among the needs most often cited were the following: counseling for parents to assist them in dealing with cultural conflicts with children, leadership training for Asian youths, knowledge of and sensitivity to special Asian feasts and celebrations, training in cultural sensitivity for teachers and catechists, and adult education programs and ESL classes for parents.

As Catholic educators we are called to participate in "the ministry of welcome" in a very special way by serving the educational needs of these Asian Americans whom we recognize and value as both culturally and spiritually enriching members of our civic communities and of our Church. It is our hope that this publication will assist all Catholic educators to understand better their Asian students, families, and neighbors—and that this understanding will in turn lead to the development of a "truly universal" Catholic community in the U.S.

Catherine T. McNamee, CSJ
President, NCEA

Report on
Asian
Hearings

Conducted by
**National Catholic Educational Association (NCEA)
United States Catholic Conference, Office of Migration
and Refugee Services (USCC/MRS)
Archdiocese of New York, Office of Pastoral Research and Planning**

October, 1989 - January, 1990

Aseries of national hearings was held from October, 1989 through January, 1990 for the purpose of listening to the pastoral and educational concerns of Asian Catholics in the United States. These hearings were held in the following dioceses: Baltimore, Boston, Chicago, Honolulu, Los Angeles, New York, Oakland, Philadelphia, Portland, San Francisco, Seattle, St. Paul/Minneapolis.

Those who gave testimony included Asian parents, Asian clergy and Asian lay ministers, and also parish and diocesan personnel who are responsible for the educational and pastoral services with the various Asian communities. Although there were many Asian groups, the primary focus of this report and project was on the following Asian communities: Chinese, Japanese, Koreans, Filipinos, Laotians (Hmong and Kmhmu), and Vietnamese.

Those who conducted the hearings were Mrs. Ruth Doyle, Director of the New York Archdiocesan Office of Pastoral Research and Planning, Rev. Peter Tran, CSsR, Special Assistant of the Office for the Pastoral Care of Migrants and Refugees, Migration and Refugee Services, USCC, and Sr. Suzanne Hall, SNDdeN, Executive Director of Special Educational Services, NCEA.

Asia and Asian Communities

Asia is an extreme continent, extreme in size, in population, in geographic features. Only a fraction of Asia's 17 million square miles is suitable for human habitation, and yet 295,000,000 people, two thirds of all the world's people, live there. The continent's mountains are the tallest in the world, and determine everything from rainfall to human life styles. They divide the land, separate people from one another, and create some of the world's most extreme geographic conditions: the hottest and coldest temperatures, the wettest lands, some of the driest deserts.

Asia has been inhabited since the earliest days of the human race. Survival in Asia's extreme climates often depended upon cooperation among an entire extended family or clan. This reliance on and reverence for family and clan still define life for many of Asia's peoples.

The Asian peoples brought the complexities of many nationalities, religions and cultural heritages with them to the United States. A consistent theme heard throughout the testimony at the hearings was that there is not one Asian community, rather many Asian communities. There are a wide variety of Asian groups, each with its own culture and language, therefore, it is not appropriate or helpful to talk about a generic "Asian" community. Respect for the significant differences among the many Asian cultures is a significant part of accepting these peoples into both society and church in the United States.

Even though this point was reiterated many times, the respondents unanimously appreciated the opportunity to come together and reflect on their experiences as "Asians", first in this country, and second, within the Catholic Church.

The Church in the Homelands

During the hearings, many people reflected on their experiences of the Catholic Church in their homeland in Asia. Their reports were of a church which was a community—a place where family and friends could experience personal warmth and caring.

The Church "at home" was viewed as hierarchical and authoritative, providing stability and a sense of order; at the same time it was perceived as *provider*, assisting a person to realize the totality of his/her being.

The Church was experienced as more traditional "at home" than in the U.S. Priests and sisters held a revered position within the community and were afforded much respect. The elders in the community were also reverenced and it is they who performed many of the leadership tasks within the parish community.

Catholic education was seen by most of the Asian respondents as desirable in their home land. The schools, generally run by missionaries, were perceived as far superior to the government schools; also, they were seen as strong evangelizers and a source of Catholic identity in an otherwise non-Christian society.

The exception to this, of course, is the Philippines, where Catholicism is very strong due to the influence of the early Spanish settlers.

The Experience of Church
in the United States

Most respondents see the United States as a place of opportunity and freedom. Thus, they believe there is the possibility of "making it" here. They see profound differences in many cultural values between the U.S. and their homelands, however, the ethic of hard work is seen as common. They want everything for their children and experience deep pain in the value clashes which are arising between themselves and their children who are being educated in U.S. schools. The importance of family as a unit is being challenged; mores around dating and sexual attitudes are quite different; the importance of the individual and the right to "self"-expression clashes with the Asian's values of deference to the elders and filial reverence.

Especially poignant were the new immigrants' and refugees' stories of their search for an experience of community within the U.S. Church, while at the same time struggling to earn a living, find shelter for their families, educate their children, and forge an identity within this new society.

The respondents reported that they experience the Church in the U.S. as unwelcoming. "Coldness" was a descriptor used on many occasions. There were many reports of attending Mass in an "American" parish and feeling totally isolated. Because Asians were accustomed to spending a great deal of time in Church, both before and after Mass, in personal and communal prayer, they find the rigid Sunday Mass schedule offensive. (An exception to this is in Hawaii where the respondents reported a tradition of welcoming all peoples, in particular the stranger. This was reported as their tradition of "Aloha".)

"Many times, we see that American Catholic people are eager to give away things such as furniture. They also sponsor newcomers, but they give the impression that they are reluctant to propose (share) Catholic faith to the newcomers."
A Southeast Asian priest

They feel that they are barely tolerated in the parish and at Mass. Many have been deeply offended by having to pay rent for a Church in order to have Mass in their native language. Also, the time set aside for their Mass was generally at an inconvenient time such as mid-afternoon on Sunday. There were many such reports during the hearings. As hard workers, they indicate that they would offer the Church far more financially than what they are being charged for rent if only the Church would welcome them and not put them in the position of being paying clients. They feel like visitors and see this as a reflection of American "big business".

A further example relating to money is the consistent report about the use of collection envelopes. Again, this is seen as offensive and bureaucratic—not a reflection of the church the respondents knew in their homelands.

There was a strong call for ethnic, pastoral "centers" which, after responding to the enculturation needs of the various Asian ethnic communities, could dissolve.

This was not a demand for national or personal parishes; to the contrary, the people voiced specific fears that such parishes might lead to separate Catholic churches within the U.S. and this was not seen as desirable by the Asian respondents. An exception to this was in the Filipino community where the representatives cited a preferrence for a recognized diocesan Filipino ministry rather than pastoral centers.

Related to this, the respondents asked for priests and ministers who speak their language(s) to minister to their communities. Especially at the time when they are new to the country, they would be grateful if the Church would be a source of comfort to them. To be able to communicate with a priest or minister in one's own language would assist in the adjustment process.

From the perspective of the Asian priests and religious, though they would not speak out publicly, many have quietly experienced deep frustration in their ministry in the U.S. They express a sense of isolation and loneliness, and a lack of support from the diocese. There were consistent calls for support groups among themselves for sharing about ministerial concerns and for socialization.

A caution was raised by some diocesan staff personnel about difficulties encountered with some Asian priests in terms of ecclesiology. In some instances, these priests have not experienced the evolution of Vatican II—its directions and practices—and there are resultant conflicts within parishes.

While, in general, the Asians' understanding of church comes out of a very traditional experience of the Catholic Church as noted above, this is not the case across the board. Catholic schools—and particularly Catholic colleges and universities in some countries—have provided their graduates with a strong grounding in the teachings of the Second Vatican Council and the call to ministry of the laity.

Expectations Re: Catholic Education in the United States

Parents stated very clear expectations of Catholic schools—education in faith, discipline, moral training, counter-cultural value system, and security—this along with a strong academic program. In addition, parents who work long hours want the school to offer supplementary programs in the early mornings and late afternoons for their children.

Asian parents want their children to retain some of their native culture and traditions, and hope that the Church here will assist them in accomplishing this goal. Because of the cultural clashes and also the fact that the children know more English than their parents in many instances, parents are reporting extreme anguish in terms of their families' future. Again, they look to the Church for assistance in this regard. The Church can be a bridge in dealing with cultural conflicts between parents and their children. Counselling sessions were suggested in many instances. The parents are not looking to the school or to social agencies to help them maintain their family units, but rather to the Church.

Relationships between individuals and their community and society are problematic. One source of strain often referred to by parents was the individualism and emphasis on self-fulfillment present in the U.S. The parents have been brought up to put the common good first—whether this is in family or society in general—to which one's own wishes become secondary. They hope to convey this sense of interdependence and responsibility for others to their children and find it difficult to do so in U.S. society.

In looking to the Church for help, the respondents noted further needs for education in the contemporary teachings of the church, in the Church's teachings regarding sexual ethics, in parenting skills, and in values clarification in our "materialistic" society. There was a strong call for religious education for both children and parents as a means for deepening their faith and assuring that they maintain it. There was also an interest in religious education for non-Catholics, especially by those parents who are the products of Catholic schooling in their homelands.

In many parishes where Asian priests are ministering to their own people, a religious education program in the native language is established. Volunteer teachers are usually the people from that ethnic group. In most instances, they are looking for assistance to update their catechetical programs. Many of these Asian communities are more familiar with the term "catechist" than with the term "religious educator." "Catechists" in their homelands are equivalent to "Directors of Religious Education" in the United States. They are people of strong faith—well respected religious leaders. In the absence of priests, they are sent out to the remote villages to gather the people in prayer and to teach catechism to adults and children. In fact, it is these lay persons who become the primary evangelizers.

Many Asians indicated that they would like to send their children to Catholic schools here, however in many instances, the expensive tuitions are beyond their ability to pay. On the other hand, however, there was an equal number of reports that, although the Catholic school was most important in their native land, the Catholic school in their new U.S. neighborhood was not viewed as on a par with the public school academically and thus was not seen as a desirable option. Asian peoples are extremely interested in the education of their children and want the very best in terms of academics as well as an atmosphere which reflects Christian values. This seems to raise the question of the role of the Catholic school in society today, especially against the backdrop of its marvelous contribution to new immigrants in the past.

A strong consensus emerged from parents who stated that they want their children to learn English in school. While they want their children to maintain the best of their culture and to become literate in their native language, they do not want the children educated in two languages in school, rather they prefer a total immersion in English.

> "*When I was in Vietnam, I was happy with one pair of thongs, two pairs of trousers. If people gave me five cents for a bowl of soup, I would be very happy. But today I have seven pairs of shoes, ten pairs of pants, and lots of other things, but I'm not happy. Happiness is not materialistic. It is a sense of time, a sense of future destination, a sense of belonging. That is why the Church is very important to me.*"
> **A Vietnamese parent**

Most school personnel and parents reported that young Asian children learn English very quickly in school—most reports indicated that in six to eight months even the new immigrants with no English are speaking and comprehending lessons taught in English.

Teachers see the Asian children as highly motivated and able students. They pay attention in class and do not create trouble. Their parents value education because they view the school as a place for academic excellence and preparation for the future. They instill that value into the children, sometimes to a fault. Some concerns were expressed that the expectations from the parents for their children to excel in school can be an added pressure on the students. In many instances, the children suffer quietly—for not living up to parent expectations.

One reservation the parents voiced was that they do not want their children to become "American", i.e., to adopt all the values of the current U.S. society. It was apparent during the hearings that the children are welcome in Catholic schools. Diocesan school office representatives indicated that they want Asian children in their schools because they are good students and do not represent any major challenge in terms of educational methodologies.

The Faith Life of the Asian people

In terms of Christianity and Catholicism, most respondents said that they saw their native spiritualities and "ways of life" (Confucianism, Buddhism, Animism and Taoism) as natural soil for the seed of their present religious beliefs. They understand that Catholicism is now a Western religion but believe that the influences of their Eastern spiritualities have had, and can continue to have, an ever-deepening and enriching effect on Catholicism as a universal religion. An exception to this is in the Filipino community. Filipino faith is largely influenced by Hispanic Catholicism.

Many respondents described how the Good News has been infused into their Eastern thought and way of life. The Confucian traditional teachings on the various levels of relationships are easily adapted to the hierarchical view of the church by Asian Catholics. The Buddhist teaching of self-purification through works of compassion is reflective of Jesus' teachings about charity. The understanding of the thirty-two spirits in Animism (for example—senses, health, happiness, identity, prosperity) is somewhat related to the experience of the Holy Spirit who breathes new life. The "way" in Taoism which is an understanding of each person in his/her nature, manner, internal law of development and wholeness, directs humankind to live with an attitude of respect, trust, and openness to the secret music of each person. The beauty of God's creation is a foundation of the Christian teaching; God creates—and sees that it is "good."

Asians want to do their faith—want to be highly involved in communal liturgies and social activities. They need to be asked to assist with parish activities; it is unseemly for an Asian to volunteer—to put oneself forward in a seemingly aggressive fashion. They believe that they have the potential to be leaders in the U.S. Church and hope to be given leadership training so they can make significant contributions to the on-going life of the Church.

It was noted on many occasions that the fundamentalist and other mainline Protestant Churches were attracting many Asian peoples, especially the new immigrants and refugees. The reasons cited for this were the welcoming attitude of these churches, the feeling of warmth and community in their services, economic and job-related assistance, English language training, and finally, the offer of leadership training and opportunities to play significant roles in those churches.

This is a significant moment in the Catholic Church's evangelization of the various Asian immigrants in this country. For the most part, Asians (Catholics and non-Catholics alike) have a very positive view of the Catholic church because of positive experiences of Catholic organizations and the work of religious orders in their homelands. There was a call to us as church to take seriously the opportunity to evangelize the many Asian immigrants who may be either Catholic or non-Catholic.

The respondents were clear that they wish to remain loyal to their Bishop; also, they are willing and anxious to use their leadership skills to develop their communities with abundant energy and commitment. They wish no confrontation and will move forward with respect. While it seemed implicit in their message that diocesan policy could assist them in their efforts, any policy which would run counter to their needs to develop would not stand in their way of creating community.

Other Sociological Considerations

The family was cited as the basic unit of society. Customarily, therefore, families, not individuals, are involved with and in church activities. This was exhibited at most of the hearings when both husband and wife attended.

In this context, an oft repeated issue had to do with the role of women in U.S. society. The respondents cited that for them the role of women is being reversed. In their native culture, the traditional roles for men and women are clearly delineated—the man is the head of the household and family, and the woman is to take care of everyone in the family before she cares for herself. However, the man does not make all the decisions, rather the woman makes many decisions regarding the home and children. The respondents used the concept of "yin/yang" to describe the complementarity of men and women in their society.

Some of the current trends in U.S. society around the role of women are putting additional strains on the Asian family. The young Asian women are questioning their traditional role as women as they take on the western values of strong self-identity, individualism, and egalitarianism. The Asian elders and men are either threatened by, or at best, confused by the beliefs and actions of the Asian woman in U.S. society. They hope that the Church and clergy can assist them in dealing with the anger and frustration related to this dynamic. The women, in turn, hope that the church can help them in dealing with their husbands' distress over their newly-found role. The strain on the family unit which arises from this conflict around role identification (in addition to the stressors of working long hours and worrying about basic livelihood) is so great that there were many calls for family counselling. This need was especially evident in situations where there are growing reports from women of physical abuse. Again, it is the church that can best respond to these calls for help because of the level of trust in this institution.

There were many reports of experiences of racial discrimination toward both Asians and Asian-Americans in the U.S. This discrimination took on various forms—being ostracized, being patronized, and being excluded from leadership roles—in both church and society. One of the more painful experiences recounted during the hearings, one which served as a backdrop to reports of discrimination, was about the struggle which the Japanese Americans had during World War II in maintaining their loyalty to the Catholic Church. After returning from the internment camps in the U.S., some Japanese reported that their churches had been closed, and in one case, literally demolished. They received no systemic support from their church, rather they experienced overt hostility and rejection.

Summary

I n summary, the Asian respondents indicated that they want a Church in which they can feel at home—where they can pray in their own language and celebrate feasts which are important to them in their homeland. As with other immigrant groups, it is important for them to have a home-base where they can feel secure before they can integrate in a healthy manner into Church and society. For this to happen it is important that diocesan policy supports and nurtures the various Asian identities. Where this has been done, particularly through ethnic centers, secure and flourishing communities have evolved.

For the most part, the Asians are not asking for long-term national/personal churches; however, they see the need for and the value of "centers" where they can worship, socialize and take part in educational opportunities in their own language. Most reports were that such "centers" would be helpful for first and second generation immigrants. These centers also offer a place to experience one's language and culture, a valuable experience for many groups who have been highly integrated into "American" society, such as the Japanese-Americans.

One parent who attended the hearings spoke eloquently about his experience of Church within U.S. society. He referred to some of the fundamentalist churches, which are making efforts to attract the new Asian immigrants, as "lakes" with well-defined boundaries and with an absolute depth. He indicated that he was not interested in responding to the very well-intentioned welcomes from these churches. In contrast, he described the Catholic Church as a "sea"—far-reaching, with constantly changing and fluid boundaries, of unknown depths, and with a capacity for a great diversity of life. It was precisely this mystery and capacity for diversity that attracted this gentleman to the Catholic Church.

The Catholic Church in the United States has the opportunity to be truly universal in its character if it will take seriously its call to accept new peoples from other lands into its community. This acceptance, however, must not be into an absolute, unchanging church; but rather, into a church that changes because of the new presence—a church whose boundaries move, whose depths are plumbed yet more, whose life of worship and community is more diverse and thus richer because of its willingness to become more truly catholic.

RECOMMENDATIONS TO CATHOLIC CHURCH AT NATIONAL AND LOCAL LEVELS

From National Hearings of Asian Catholic Communities in the United States

January, 1990

The major call was for acknowledgement of the voice of the Asian communities within the church in the United States through the following actions:

- A National Convocation of representatives of Asian Catholic communities in the U.S.;
- The naming of an Asian Bishop in the U.S.;
- A National Pastoral Letter on the Asian Presence in the U.S.

In addition, the respondents at the hearings offered many recommendations to Church ministers and educators. The following represent those most often cited as needs:

1. Welcoming committees within parishes;
2. "Centers" where liturgies, etc. can take place in native language;
3. Counseling for parents to assist them in dealing with cultural conflicts with children;
4. Leadership training for Asians, especially for youth;
5. Language training for teachers, priests, and ministers;
6. Knowledge of and sensitivity to special Asian feasts and celebrations by priests and ministers;
7. After-school programs for children of parents who work; also, family programs and socials sponsored by parish;
8. Training in cultural sensitivity for clergy, educators and ministers;
9. Adult education programs for parents, especially ESL classes;
10. Financial assistance to enable children to attend Catholic schools;
11. Ethnic studies in Catholic schools; curricular adaptations to reflect Eastern traditions, cultures;
12. Recruitment of Asian teachers and catechists;
13. Training of laity to be catechists and ministers of various types in parish/ diocese;
14. Cultural awareness and language training in seminaries;
15. National Directory of catechetical materials available in various languages;
16. Acceptance of Asian peoples on parish and diocesan policy-making bodies.

CHAPTER I

History, Culture and Religious Expression

CHINA

China is the largest country in Asia, covering approximately 1/14th of the world's land. Its population represents 1/5th to 1/4th of the world's total. Chinese call their country Chung-Kuo—Central Kingdom—because earlier Chinese thought they were the center of civilization. The name "China" was given by people from other countries and may have originated from the name "Ch'in", the ruler who united China from several smaller warring states between 221 - 210 B.C. and named himself the First Sovereign Emperor (Shih-Huang-Ti). Scientists believe the Peking Man, dating back a million years, was an early Chinese ancestor.

China is one of the oldest living civilizations dating back 3500 years. A well established Chinese way of life was formed probably earlier than the Chou period (circa 1100-722 B.C.), and surely by the era of the Warring States (402-221 B.C.). Ancient Chinese encouraged education. Traditionally, educated officials had been much more respected by the people than were warriors. Confucian social order led to civilized human relationships: King—Ministers, Father—Son, Husband—Wife, Brothers—Sisters etc., emphasizing government by virtue. Subjects should be loyal; rulers should lead exemplary lives, and inspire their subjects to be good. Children should have filial piety, but parents should be loving. Friends should be faithful to each other, thus, there would be peace and prosperity.

Mencius, one of the later interpreters of Confucius, warned rulers of how their power emanates from the people and the lack of their consent might justify a rebellion. Taoists opposed Confucian interference in formulating rigorous rules and regulations of life and advocated respect for human nature by following the Way (TAO) to preserve one's life: "Good fortune and calamity alternate"; "In order to take, one first gives." Social philosophies flourished, one complementary to another.

Legalism flourished in the Ch'in period, enabling the ruler to be effective and making the country strong. Legalists believed that evil human nature was controllable only by harsh laws, and they advocated uniform and strict punishment to eliminate selfishness, without regard to rank or status. Ch'in in effect unified the Warring States. But legalist laws were so harsh and strict that the people soon rebelled and the Ch'in dynasty lasted only a short time.

Confucianism taught an ethical system, while Taoism taught people how to rise above suffering and calamity. However, neither offered solace for pain and mortality. Buddhism was introduced to China in the Han dynasty (206 B.C. to 221 A.D.) teaching deliverance from misery, old age, sickness and death. By the T'ang period (618-907 A.D.) the greatest thinkers were the Buddhist monks.

The Chinese are proud of their nation and its influence on world history. Their creativity in arts and inventions produced elaborate vases, outstanding paintings, enamel wares of famous design which required advanced firing methods, astronomy, map-making, paper invention and refinement, printing, gun powder, compass discoveries and their use, introduction of silk cloth, paper money, and means of travel.

Two successful foreign invasions took place—the Mongols (1289-1368 A.D.) and the Manchus (1644-1911). The former did not last long and the latter had to assimilate Chinese language and culture to survive. From the 7th to the 10th centuries (T'ang Period), China was in its golden era. Between the 14th and 16th centuries, China became an indisputable world power. Chinese civilization developed and prospered without the influence of Old Testament or Christianity. Above all, it emerged singularly outside of Greco-Roman cultures.

For several centuries, Christian missionaries, disguised by engaging in secular activities, had sought acceptance in the Central Kingdom. After the last dynasty was overthrown in 1911, all forms of contact quickly increased between China and

> "*A*sians who were immigrants to this country usually have their own problems such as employment, housing, and medical care requiring their immediate attention. As a result, they just do not have time or interest to come to the church for Sunday masses or other activities. In the circumstance, it would be good for the church, whenever possible, to introduce some relevant social services to those Catholics who are newcomers to this country, especially to those who would come from Hong Kong."
> **A Chinese community leader**

the outside world. Chinese have been coming to the West to learn technology and science. Missionaries found education to be one of the better means of evangelization and established many secular schools in various missions. But Chinese intellectuals remain indifferent to alien religious belief. Modern missionaries would be better prepared if Chinese conventional values and Confucian attitudes were incorporated into their formative training.

The Selection of the Able and the Worthy

In ancient China, an educational arrangement gradually developed from the system of Imperial Civil Service Examination, later called the Han-Lin Imperial Academy. It was entirely based on knowledge of Chinese classics. Thus, a characteristic elite was formed by private preparatory study which flourished throughout China among the Han-Lin competitors. It continued uninterrupted, dynasty after dynasty, until its abolition in 1905.

The arrangement enabled people to pass the Imperial Examination, gain an appointment to a governmental office, and enjoy its associated trust and honor and it enabled the Court to selectively "employ the able and promote the worthy." Confucian classics became synonymous with basic social values in imperial China. Learning was purely mnemonic and had a literary, philosophical and ethical nature. The system gave commoners an equal opportunity to become high ranking officials. The concern was centered on training political technicians who could act as advisers to rulers and leaders. General citizenry acquired their job skills by working with and imitating family elders in every trade, and learning crafts through apprenticeship. For many, the private arrangement of education was unaffordable. The expressiveness of creativity, thinking and behavior was inhibited because what Confucianism did not teach was not considered necessary.

An Agrarian Civilization

Confucian social order led to civilized human relationships and established a Chinese way of life. The Kingdom developed and expanded. A Transport Canal (589-618 A.D.) was dug to link the lower Yangtse River with the middle reaches of the Yellow River (Huang-ho), far longer than the Panama and Suez canals combined. A gigantic monumental Great Wall was also erected, along the northern defense line. Both required untold human sacrifices. The establishment of provinces with civil and military governors directly responsible to the Emperor, a network of roads, coinage, weights, measure standardization, irrigation system (206-220 B.C.), travel and trade, and the introduction of Buddhism across the Himalaya mountains made China a well settled agrarian society. By the T'ang era (618-907 A.D.), a proliferation of arts, literature and handicrafts had reached the unimmaginable. By the Ming dynasty (1368-1644 A.D.), China assumed oceanic hegemony, reaching out to Java, Ceylon, the Persian Gulf and Africa, and de-

3

manded tributes and submissive recognition from the "barbarians" outside the Central Kingdom.

Proud Chinese Literati Officials

Confucian culture kept a vast society relatively stable through the ages. Confucian order became deeply rooted as the norm of Chinese life. The elite class emerged from life-long schooling in Confucian traditions and values. Their social standing and esteem depended considerably on their identification with these traditions and values. The Central Kingdom was in a state of self-sufficiency and self-esteem to the point of imposing *kowtow* on whomever it came in contact with. This may be likened to the post-Theodosius II era (401-450) in Europe of seeming religious monopoly, an era ruled by ecclesiastical edicts exhibiting intolerance of dissent from Christianity. In China, all means of education were developed and used to strengthen Church authority for more than a thousand years (5th-15th century). Education emphasized an obedient acceptance of the authority of revealed truth. Reason and knowledge were subservient to theology. The Imperial Examination System, according to which the ruling elite were chosen, reinforced these Confucian principles.

Foreign Influence and Educational Reform

The Examination system was modified only in 1898 by adding "knowledge of things going on outside China." It was abolished in 1905 with the promise of new reform. The Peking National University (Peita) was opened in 1898 and began non-Confucian studies. Annually, thousands of students were sent to Japan, the U.S. and Europe to learn western science and technology. Returnees played an important role in government decisions.

From foreign commercial interests came all forms of foreign ideas. The public educational system, promised earlier, was introduced in China in the new Republic following the overthrow of the last dynasty in 1911. The modern educational system was patterned after the Western model. Mass book-learning was established. Many of the revolutionaries studied overseas or had contacts with foreign educational systems or civilizations. The new system was instituted by districting, and was controlled and supported by the community, either by tuition or by government direct financing. Once a privilege of the few, education was to become a right of the many.

The May 4, 1919 movement led by Hu-shih reformed the language style using plain colloquial writings (Bai-huah) to help many in reading and writing, and eliminated ancient classics from lower schools. Attention also was drawn to the importance of attacking and removing illiteracy through the Popular Education. Textbook materials specially designed for peasants and workers were widely distributed by James Yen, a well known champion of mass education, to teach basic reading and writing.

Secondary and technical schools were added to train men and women for the multitude of posts pressingly needed in an infancy of industrialization. Curriculum was broadened to include Foreign Language, World History, Geography, Math, Geometry, Algebra, Chemistry, Physics and Biology. Institutes of higher learning for research and study were established. While the accent was on science and technology in the new Republic, the ruling party, Kuomingtang, imposed democratic ideology as a mandatory course in every field of learning, in all schools, including higher learning institutes.

Status of Education in 1948

Unfortunately, the new Republic, headed by Kuomingtang (Nationalist), had to confront regional sedition at the outset, conflict with Japan later, interparty squabbles and fighting. Finally, aggravated by corruption among officials, it collapsed in 1949 after losing the civil war to the communists. The residual Nationalist forces fled to Taiwan. Yet progress had been made, considering China was made up of five major cultural groups, scores of principal dialects, an area of 3,691,523 square miles and an estimated population of 500,000,000 in 1948. At the height of civil war, less than 30 years after the radical educational innovations, there were more than 200 universities and institutions of higher learning, a faculty of 20,000, an enrollment of 155,000 (of which 25,000 graduated yearly). There were 6,000 secondary schools (grades 7 to 12), 140,000 teachers, 2 million students and 400,000 graduates each year. There were also 300,000 primary schools (grades 1 to 6), 785,000 teachers, about 24 million pupils, and nearly 5 million graduates yearly. It was estimated that 20 percent of school-age children attended primary and secondary schools at the time.[1] Catholics and Protestants were contributing to the effort by running thousands of schools and scores of universities, including some of the most prestigious.

PRC Application of Marxist Dialectics in Education

The Peoples Republic of China (PRC) began manipulating print and visual media in the 1950s. The Chinese Communist Party launched a mass campaign to use education for political goals. The dominating concern was to produce graduates to ensure the people's political reliability. There was a stream of zig-zag ideological mood changes: the 1956-57 PRC support for the Hundred Flowers Campaign was reversed in 1958-1960 by the Great Leap Forward Campaign, a condemnation of the Rightist Deviation, followed by an unexpected relaxation concerning artistic and intellectual expression in 1962. In 1963, the PRC reminded its people to place political agenda ahead of artistic criteria and academic endeavors. The Great Proletarian Cultural Revolution, from 1966 to 1976, brought an intolerant policy toward past heritage. Teenage Red Guards attacked all remnants of traditional China, annihilating all vestiges of old culture. The movement was derisively renamed "cultural involution." Political activism replaced formal schooling during this period. Public education was shut down, and the students were dispatched to the countryside. Earlier in the 1950s, private and missionary schools had been confiscated and foreign faculties expelled.

Between 1976 and 1989, prior to the May-June 1989 events on Tiananmen Square, a great number of graduate students had gone abroad to further their study in the U.S., Japan and Europe. From province to province, the schools gradually resumed their activities around 1976 as before the cultural revolution.

Status of Education in PRC

By 1987 in China, there were 210 million Chinese pupils enrolled in 164,000 kindergartens, 900,000 primary schools, 160,000 secondary schools and 633 institutes of higher learning. Of the 94% of children enrolled in primary schools, only about 40% went on to finish secondary school. Only about 6% of university applicants gained admissions. In short, about 2-3% of Chinese youth entered college compared to 40% of the U.S. youth. For post-graduate training, only 14 out of every 1,000 applicants gained a place.[2]

School curricula emphasized political content at the expense of academic work. A few years ago, in the Kweichow Province, the estimate was as follows: 58% of lessons devoted to Maoist thought and class struggle; 21% learning from workers (manual labor) and 21% basic academic subjects. Academic works included foreign language, arithmetic, writing in Chinese, handicraft, drawing and music, nature studies, history, geography and physics in secondary schools. Marxism was imposed on all people by the proletariat dictatorship, which was still fully backed by the military appointees.

Traditional Culture
Survived Outside PRC

Vis-a-vis the destructive educational policy in Mainland China, a reformed system continues to prosper in Taiwan as planned at the founding of the Republic. Today, Taiwan's achievement in economic development and scientific technology has been largely attributed to the government's emphasis on education. The number of Taiwanese overseas students is second to none, though the Island is only a small part of China (with only 20 million people).

Chinese people in the diaspora have a long tradition of maintaining their proud heritage. Wherever a large settlement is seen, a Chinese school can be found to preserve the traditional language and to enrich the people with their ancient culture. The legacy of Imperial Examination lives on pervasively: with an education, one may rise above one's emigre status; without it, one surely will be bound to stay put.

Earlier Chinese In America

Many old and new speculations exist about when and how the Chinese first reached the U.S. There was a well documented Chinese student who came to Yale College in 1847. He graduated later and returned to China. In those years, China had just suffered a devastating defeat during the Opium War against Britain, which radically eroded Chinese pride and self-esteem. Many revolutionary Chinese were calling for modernization and the overthrow of the Manchu dynasty. The military might of the British Navy surprised Chinese officials and provoked a strong nationalistic demand in China for learning Western science and technology.

The hardship of post-war life created an impetus to search for a better livelihood elsewhere. Groups of hard-pressed laborers living on the southeastern seashore of China were captivated by American Gold Rush stories and lured by some unscrupulous operators of ocean liners. Most of these emigrants reached the Southeast Asian countries: the Philippines, Indonesia, Thailand, Vietnam and Malaysia. Today there are 15 to 20 million Chinese who live and work in that region. Others went to California's "Mountain of Gold" (Gum-Shan). By 1851, some 25,000 Chinese had been recruited to the West Coast, becoming the main labor force to build the Transcontinental Railroad, Northwest Pacific, and Southern Pacific links. They constituted one tenth of American farm labor in 1870.

Brutalities Against Chinese Workers

The numbers of Chinese immigrants to the U.S. increased as the economy prospered and expanded. These laborers did not intend to settle permanently in the U.S. The Confucian dictate imbued their minds: " So long as parents live, (sons) travel not afar." They intended solely to earn wages to take back to China. Unfortunately, economic downturn caused whites to blame the Chinese for taking their jobs. An Immigration Law was passed in 1882 prohibiting further Chinese entry. Those Chinese who were permitted to stay suffered a succession of brutal laws against them: they were not allowed to become U.S. citizens, to intermarry, or to own land. They could not bring their families in China to the U.S., and they lived lonely lives. Patent hostility toward Chinese would have been more understandable, had there been a really threatening wave of Chinese immigrants in such an inhospitable climate. Historically, in 1885, 1886 and 1887—the years preceding the 1888 Exclusion Act of Scott—only 22, 40, and 10 Chinese entered the U.S., respectively. It was hardly a case of the Chinese living on public welfare. The dislike had to originate from the inherent nature of racial prejudice and discrimination against ethnic Chinese-ness. In a "one man one vote" constitutional democracy, the cry of the minuscle number of Chinese was too weak to be heard in political circles. Cruel treatment was rampant in housing and public places. Special taxes were levied selectively on occupations the Chinese were most likely to take. They were excluded from mining and fishing and had practically no choice but to take

7

unwanted jobs such as farming, digging, washing, ironing, cooking and serving food. They finally established laundries and restaurants. Dr. B.L. Sung, one of the foremost experts on the Chinese in America, put it this way: "Murdering Chinese became such a commonplace occurence that the newspapers seldom bothered to print the stories. ...The indignities, abuses, brutalities and injustices practiced against the Chinese were outrageous."[3]

Chinese-Americans of The New Era

The Chinese Exclusion Act was repealed only in 1943 when the U.S. aligned itself with China in World War II. A quota of 105 Chinese each year was then allowed by immigration law until 1965, when the new liberalized Immigration Act was adopted. Chinese immigrants increased rapidly during the past twenty years, as did all other Asians: 47% of immigrants entering the U.S. in 1986 were of Asian ancestry. The 1980 census reported over 806,000 ethnic Chinese in the U.S.; that number is expected to total 1.3 million in the 1990 census.

> "*In general all immigrants expect a better life in the U.S. than their old country. Furthermore, they expect a better life for their children and their family. The better life includes the freedom, the working conditions, the freedom to worship, the equality, the education, the security and stability, the food and housing.*"
>
> **A Chinese parish minister**

The overwhelming majority of Chinese immigrants of the past came from Southern China, Toishan, near Canton. Many of these merchants, laborers, tradesman and farmers were unfamiliar with the English language and American culture, and many were illiterate in their native language. Often they were afflicted by an inferiority complex, behaving in a docile and eager manner to avoid conflicts in the hope of "fitting in." They tended to congregate in Chinatown ghettos or in other clusters of Asians depending on their spoken dialect. The stereotypic public images of Chinese consisted of men in opium dens, the cunning and devious Fu-Manchu, and hair tied in pigtails. Their nostalgic love for the homeland and longing for their children's betterment made them the strongest among the Chinese subgroups in retaining their traditions.

American-born Chinese are abandoning the laundry and restaurant businesses and have gone on to all professions seeking equal integration in American society. They are scattered throughout the U.S. and tend to reside outside Chinatown. Many of them do not speak Chinese and have limited knowledge of Chinese culture. Their ties with China are weak and gradually diminishing. However, old perceptions based on their physical appearance sometimes still affect them.

The majority of new Chinese immigrants are coming from Taiwan and Hong-Kong. Some are coming from the mainland since diplomatic relations were re-established. Many of these later groups escaped political and ideological persecutions. Most speak Mandarin besides their own dialects. Many of the new immigrant Chinese are well educated, more sophisticated and financially better off than the earlier groups. Many have a working knowledge of English. These groups live mostly in metropolitan Asian clusters outside the Chinatowns.

Although there are differences in spoken Cantonese, Toishanese, Hakka and Mandarin, Chinese writing remains one and the same for all dialect-speaking people. Mandarin-speaking Chinese come from North and Central China, the cradle of Chinese civilization. Many are sympathetic to the PRC because of its clout in international affairs, particularly after President Carter's recognition of the PRC in 1978. Traditional associations in Chinatown are uncomfortable with the new social service organizations operated with U.S. government funding. As always, there is a gap between the old and the new immigrant groups.

In recent years, both American-born and other educated Chinese scholars have been using publications and social research studies to clear up stereotypical Chinese images. There are more than a dozen Chinese dailies on the newstands of New York's Chinatown alone. Many street demonstrations organized by the Chinese are occurring over a variety of social issues. For example, a few years ago an estimated 20,000 Chinese demonstrated against an addition to the prison compound in the midst of New York City's Chinatown.

In many churches, special evangelization efforts are being planned or carried out for and with Asians, many with the valuable assistance of Asian clergy. The vitality of some of these ethnic Churches is phenomenal when compared with the years prior to the 1965 immigration law. Now, one can hardly distinguish a Church service in a U.S. Chinatown from one in Hong Kong or Taiwan. Chinese Christians are few in number and work long hours, which limits their participation in church activities. Some recruiting efforts should be discussed in pastoral circles. Many Asian clergy, being immigrants themselves, need considerable assistance and adaptation to local church customs and traditions.

Educational Concerns Of Chinese Immigrants

C hildren's education is an overiding common endeavor among Chinese families. By and large, local school authorities do not reach out to help the immigrant families or they do so in a less than sensitive manner, for example, having no translator or childcare at counseling conferences. The children, with a knowledge of English, act frequently as translators for their parents and have to deal with their family problems: be it the rent, telephone bills, a business problem or the children's school performance, problems many families would normally discuss in their children's absence to avoid burdening them. Many influences and contributions from the Asians are willfully omitted in school lessons on account of well-known historical prejudices. Some teachers would try to dissuade the Chinese pupils from speaking Chinese. It's widely known how these children try to hide and deny their own Asian-ness by pleading with their parents not to speak the native language in the company of their peers. Other children sometimes ridicule newly-arrived immigrants. Low self-esteem has been cited often to rationalize the passivity of many Asian students' class participation and their poor self-image. To Asian students applying for college, a guidance counselor may not present career opportunities other than math and science or may simply discourage them from exploring outside these fields. These Asian students may be disadvantaged by evaluations depicting them as introverted and narrowly focused. Even local-born Chinese who think and act like Americans will not be accepted entirely among American peers as one of their own kind. The children of Asian immigrants need their own kind to round out their feeling of belonging and security. Physical appearance, isolation and limited English proficiency become racial barriers.

Immigrant Chinese parents find themselves in a quandary in having to choose a balance between strict upbringing of children according to their heritage and holding back their children's Americanization. Announcements on school bulletin boards, television or radio often fail to reach the parents. This is a painful experience for which many families desperately seek guidance. In most schools an insufficient number of Asian students precludes a bilingual class setting or recruitment of a trained Asian student counselor.

Education as Means of Evangelization Among Chinese

World-wide human resources and cultures are rapidly assuming global significance with the advent of international trade, satellite TV, supersonic transport and liberalization of immigration policy in many countries. This has already awakened the conscience of many in sharing the blessings of nature, in encouraging a better integration of diverse cultures and in promoting democracy and freedom. Many U.S. education officials are calling for greater appreciation of our ethnic, cultural and linguistic differences and are proposing substantive curriculum changes.

Christians from China are deeply grateful for the evangelical efforts of Christians from all over the world, particularly the Americans during the 1930s and the 1940s. In mainland China, religious schools were completely closed down and all missionaries were expelled in the early 1950s. China's atheistic regime relaxed its hold on some religious practices and repaired many Christian churches in the years between 1978 and 1989. However, any missionary endeavor, either pastoral or secular, seems far from getting the PRC's understanding, unless efforts are totally independent from foreign connection and entirely under the so called "Patriotic Church" control. In mainland China, traditional Chinese culture and way of life are also undergoing a tremendous communist transformation to the point of losing Chinese identity.

In the province of Taiwan, and in the soon-to-be-returned Hong Kong territory, foreign religious participation in education still continues to flourish among Chinese people. Chinese in Taiwan, Hong Kong and many Chinese immigrant communities all over the world, including those in the United States, are awaiting the same kind of evangelical commitment. These converts may well be the seeds of tomorrow's Christianity on the Chinese mainland. Education has been valued as one of the better means of evangelization among Chinese Confucianists, detached from foreign religions. Wherever a public system of education performs poorly, a non-Christian Chinese family may seek enrollment of their children in a parochial school which enjoys a reputation of seriousness and success among Chinese. Through education, many non-Christian families come in contact and keep dialogue with Christian religion. Educational activity has been perceived by missionaries as a resistance-lowering means in acculturation too. In this context, Christian education is facing a real challenge in the United States, with the ever increasing numbers and diversity of immigrants.

Confucian Attitudes and Religious Antagonism

Christian evangelization has never been easy in China. From the earliest Jesuit missionaries in the 1580s to the communist takeover in 1949, there were only approximately three million Catholics and fewer than one million Protestants. The massive unresponsiveness of the Chinese educated class to Christianity cannot be understood without another detailed analysis. The *literati* officials in the past vehemently resented any disdain toward their way of life. Historically, China had been tolerant of Buddhism and Islam, both of foreign origin, yet Emperor Yung-cheng prohibited the Christian religion in 1724 as a heterodox, forbidden sect with a connotation of political and social subversiveness. Today, evangelization efforts are centering on the integration of Confucianism with Christian faith and making earnest accommodations. Many missionaries are presenting the Bible and the Christian faith avoiding the arrogant air of absolute incontrovertibility. Church officials no longer denounce Chinese ancestral traditions or culture. Members of the Chinese educated class are approaching the Christian faith with philosophical curiosity and uncovering diversity which complements Chinese traditions. Alienation and antagonism of yesterday are now replaced by inquisitive interests.

Cultural Differences and Christianity Customs

The church's involvement in the Chinese community has provided vitally needed social services, such as the education of children, multi-cultural adaptation, immigration and business liasons. Understanding the Confucian mentality should facilitate communication between the traditional Chinese and the Christians. To light a candle makes no sense to a Chinese person, just as the burning of an incense stick may be ridiculous for an average American. "All Souls' Day" would be more meaningful when ancestors are remembered at the *Ching-ming* (sweeping tombs) worship festival. Abstinence from meat on Fridays would also be quite understandable if Buddhist vegetarian days in the lunar calendar were respected too. A Chinese couldn't agree more with the Christians in refuting the notion that "this is my body, it's entirely up to me...." The concept of parental origin as gift and love is more than enough to convince a Chinese to preserve it—body and reputation as integral part of the family—as best one can. The swearing over an unknown and culturally irrelevant Bible is considered outlandish by Chinese, particularly if the local practices are willfully ignored; the constant emphasis on individual freedom has not been looked upon with favor if a clan's collective stake is not also mentioned; the adoration of God does not exclude ancestral veneration.

There are other seemingly contradictory Christian behaviors like the cry of female discrimination, while scant attention is paid to pedestals reserved for the mothers in Chinese families; the community propitiation to gods for rain in times of droughts is condemned by Christians while a prayerful Christian procession is held for the same intention. The erection of ostentatious and incongruent cathedral compounds is a total disregard of Chinese geomantic notions (Feng-shui). Many Christian customs associated with the holidays, (Christmas, Easter, Sundays, feasts of obligation, etc.), having no exact counterparts in Chinese culture, are viewed with popular fear and suspicion. Sermons are preached based on histories of saints totally unfamiliar to the Chinese while abundant Chinese anecdotes of heroes of loyalty and faithfulness, of love and personal sacrifices, of the teachings of Confucius and Laotze predating Christianity are considered sacrilegious. This insistence on exclusion alienates Chinese rather than attracting them.

Expanded Horizons
of Chinese Converts

It is refreshing to bring Christian activism to the Chinese way of life. The Confucian dictum "Do not do to others what you would not want others to do unto you" sounds peaceful but passive. Listening to Christ's "love your neighbors as yourself.., enemy, ...lepers, lowly and abandoned, sinners and convicts, etc.," one feels exhorted and ready to act. Many saintly Catholics who were called by their faith offered their energies and lives, left their families, and abandoned all secular aspirations to go to distant mission lands, some with full knowledge of never returning home. Many of them have deeply touched strangers from foreign lands. It is not a question of superiority or belittling one idea or another. The Confucian concept of expanding the love and harmony horizontally across societal relations, from the closest to the farthest, from one village to other villages, remains strictly an interpersonal one, tangible and visible. The Christian doctrine of "neighbor" was detailed by Jesus himself in the parable of the Good Samaritan. It is not the closeness that counts but the needs and sufferings we come in contact with. A real life example: A successful Catholic industrialist of Milan, Italy, sold everything in his prime of entrepreneurial activity in the 1960s, went to the Amazon jungle of Brazil and built a hospital and health care stations for lepers. A Confucian Chinese might ask why he didn't just as well do the same good in his own slums of Milan or Naples. Dr. M. Candia's startling answer was: "Why should love be limited to here or there? If that becomes the case, there isn't any more charity." These strange "neighbors" are the very people comprised in the outer perimeter of the Confucian "love" command: "Love my own family-connections and go on loving the family-connections of others...."

Chinese youth today witnessed in bitter rage the Tiananmen massacre of June 4, 1989. They yearn for justice and human solidarity. There should be more than just a Confucian question of "why should one speculate on the after-life when the life at hand is still poorly understood?" In the Christian faith, Chinese will find a reassuring solace for pain and suffering. The immortal valor of these young students will live beyond our generation, just as the splendid martyrs in Catholic faith are inscribed in the Church's annals. Christians actively and positively seek discussion of immortality while alive and propose to sanctify their lives to gain eternal beatitude.

The ultimate sacrifices of the youth in Tiananmen Square should teach the living much more than "sweep away the snow on one's own front step, interfere not with the frost on others' rooftops." It is time to instill in Confucian minds the sense of justice in Christianity and elevate the meaning of ethereal life.

Some Christians often spoke up on behalf of the Chinese, such as during the persecution and anti-Chinese riots in California, and objected to laws barring "coolies" from America by voicing alarm about Chinese male laborers "without women and children, living like animals on the plantations." This reality may not delete the dark chapter of the Chinese Exclusion history of which the most vociferous proponents came from the Workingmen's Party, mainly composed of Irish and Southern European Catholics. It does, however, impress all Chinese that fair-minded Catholics and missionaries do exist. Sometimes, they prominently confront very unpopular issues at their own peril with righteousness and justice. After all, Confucian virtues can easily find equivalents in Catholic conscience.

U.S. Policy Towards Chinese Exchange Students

In the U.S. today, there are more than 40,000 Chinese graduate students, thousands of whom are returning to their homeland with a knowledge of western cultures and religion. Though many remain disinterested in Christianity, few would ever contemplate hostile harassment against the Christian faith. They are future friends of Western democracy. Thousands of Chinese graduates from Christian institutions of higher learning are contributing to the national reconstruction or going on to excel in their fields of studies, totally free of accepting any religious belief. Nevertheless, Christian education will remain with them.

Prospects of Christianity in China

The last fifty years of "proletarian dictatorship" gave Chinese people one of the most monolithic educational systems known to them. In spite of whatever rancor the Chinese may have had toward the Christian religion, evangelical teachings brought a kind of eclectic yet peaceful enrichment to an old culture. Missionary schools bridged the initial gap between human civilization and Divine Truth. The process was spiritually positive and economically constructive. Chinese people are becoming increasingly receptive to Christian beliefs, and the prospect for the future is much brighter.

Footnotes

1. D.P. Whitaker et al. *Area Handbook for the Peoples Republic of China*, PAS of American University, 1972.
2. Fodor's *Peoples Republic of China Travel Guide*, 1987.
3. B.L. Sung. *The Story of the Chinese in America*, Collier Books, New York, NY.

References

1. *Twenty Centuries of Education*, Edgar W. Knight, Ginn & Co., Boston, 1940.
2. *The Cambridge History of China*, Vol. 10, Part 1.
3. *Asian-American Concerns*, N.Y.C. Board of Ed., Chancellor's Task Force Report, 1989.
4. *Old Traditions, New Directions: Chinese Heritage and Culture*, Board of Ed., New York, NY, Jan., 1990.
5. *Strangers From A Different Shore*, Ronald Takaki, Little Brown, 1989.

ASIAN-INDIAN CATHOLICS:
Serving the Future
by Understanding the Past

Asian Indians suddenly began appearing on the west coast of the United States in 1907, but this period of early Asian-Indian immigration was extremely short. Immigration officials began placing restrictions in 1909 and Congress prohibited immigrants from India eight years later. Altogether, only 6,400 came to the United States. By 1940, according to the U.S. Census, the Asian-Indian population in the United States had increased to only 2,405—a small and stable community, most of whom were elderly, uneducated, farmers or farm laborers; 60 percent resided in California; only four percent were professionals; and of the 1,600 under 25 years of age, more than a third had not completed even a year of schooling. Compared to all the racial and ethnic groups reported that year in the census, the educational level of Asian Indians was the lowest, with only 3.7 median number of school years completed.[1]

This situation has changed dramatically since 1965, with the removal of the Asian Exclusion Act and new immigration legislation: by 1980 the United States population included 387,223 Asian Indians. Still, the number of immigrants arriving from India has never been as large as the number coming from other Asian countries such as China, South Korea, or the Philippines.

Indian Catholics
in the United States

Asian-Indian Catholics in the United States today are not a community with deep roots in America. The early immigrants came from the fertile plains of the Punjab, and most of the migrants were Sikhs. Asian-Indian Catholics did not arrive in any numbers until the mid 1960s.

The number of Asian-Indian Catholic immigrants remains extremely small. This should not be surprising. Although Catholics in India constitute the second largest Catholic community in Asia after the Philippines, in relative numbers it comprises a mere fraction of India's 840 million people. Christians in India represent 2.6 percent of the total population; Catholics, about 1.6 percent. No matter how many more Asian-Indians arrive in this country, only a small proportion will be Catholic.

The bulk of these immigrants arriving since the mid 1960s are under 40 years of age. In large part this is due to the new and more restrictive qualifications demanded of those wishing to come to the United States from third-world countries. These more recent immigrants are thus part of the national elite: fairly Westernized, urban, middle or upper-middle class—and certainly not economically deprived. They come for reasons of professional advancement (doctors, engineers, etc.) or further education. After they have established themselves, they gradually send for their extended families, who are not subject to the same restrictive immigration requirements. Over the next two decades, then, the Indian Catholic community in the United States will consist of a core of professional or semi-professional men and women and students, whose numbers will continue to increase. Added to this group will be a second ring of less-educated and occupationally less-skilled people, often less urban and not very Westernized, who have come principally because of their blood relationships with the core group.

What is the Catholic cultural context from which these Asian-Indians come? To answer this question requires some understanding of the reality and history of the Catholic Church in India.[2]

Catholic Church in India

Despite its size (about 14 million) and its ancient roots, Catholicism remains a minority religion in India and exhibits neither cultural homogeneity nor uniform jurisdiction. It contains both Westernized Catholics and tribal members, Roman as well as the Syro-Malabar and Syro-Malankara rites. Nor are Catholics evenly distributed geographically. Kerala, with almost 4 percent of the nation's population and its highest literacy rate, contains almost 40 percent of India's Catholic population. The vast heartland of the subcontinent—Uttar Pradesh, Madya Pradesh and Bihar—which represents the political base of the government and the civil bureaucracy, has very few Catholics at all.

Catholics in India do not speak a common language or share common customs. Except in Kerala, where the Syrian Christians are a landholding class wielding considerable power in the state's economic and political life, the only unifying element among Indian Catholics is that they mostly belong to the economically middle and lower classes. Despite this relative poverty, the Catholic community owns and manages a vast complex of more than 14,000 educational, medical, cultural and charitable institutions. Its school system in particular has made a conspicuous contribution both to the Church's excellent relations with the educated non-Christian elite majority and to the prestige and social standing of the Catholic clergy. Ironically, the very success of the schools, which have educated so many non-Christian Indians and may have been the most important conduit for the liberal ideas embodied in India's Constitution, has also contributed to perceptions of Catholicism as an ally, if not an agent, of a foreign colonial culture and an unwitting promoter of cultural dependency. Such contrasts only complicate the task of understanding the heterogeneous Catholic community in India.

The complexity of Indian Catholicism is best approached through its history. According to common belief, Christianity came to India with the Apostle Thomas. He was martyred in Mylapore, near the city of Madras, and his room is preserved there, where it is an object of pious veneration. Although the historical evidence to support this belief is shaky, there is clear evidence that from the 4th century a substantial native Christian community existed on the Malabar coast in southern India. This group, called the Syrian (or St. Thomas) Christians, restricted to the extreme southwest of the Indian peninsula, neither penetrated the larger subcontinent nor challenged the prevalent Hindu movements that grew up on the very same soil. Until the Portuguese arrived in 1498, the St. Thomas Christians were living in two worlds: the political and social world of the Malabar coast and the ecclesiastical world that was more or less Chaldean in character. Chaldean prelates governed them in spiritual matters, and they shared the theological, juridical and liturgical traditions of the Chaldean Church.

The Portuguese brought Latin Christianity to India, even though the arrival of the Franciscans and Dominicans in the two previous centuries had inevitably provided some exposure to it and some exchange of ideas. With the Portuguese came secular priests, more Franciscans, and the Jesuits, who eventually established themselves as the missionary stalwarts of the East. Historians have usually seen this exporting of Latin Christianity to India as an integral part of the expansion of European power in the early modern period. This power had commercial, military, political and ideological dimensions. Thus, merchants, soldiers, administrators and priests all combined to further Western interests and to challenge "traditional" India on a wide front.

But there is another perspective in which East and West, modern or traditional, victory or defeat, are not so easy to distinguish. From this viewpoint, the Portuguese came not as conquerors, but as another element in an already complex mosaic. As participants rather than as conquerors, they had services to render and benefits to receive. They were welcomed as allies by some, but they needed allies in return.

The Church's religious activities could be seen in a similar way. Influence and accommodation seem much more appropriate than spiritual conquest to describe the growth of Christianity after 1498, especially after Portuguese political power began to wane early in the 17th century. Christianity was offered to the Paravas tribes on the Fishery Coast at the precise moment when they needed Portuguese protection for secular reasons, and they constructed a Christian community that resembled a Hindu caste. Accommodation as well as persecution characterized

> "*The Church should first address the issue of immigrant priests. They need to be welcomed; they need help in the orientation class; they need to be reminded of their vocation. The future of the Church here is through the new immigrants.*"
> **An Indian educator**

17

relations between the clergy and the Brahmins of Goa. The guiding principle given by the Vatican to its first departing papal vicars to India in the early 17th century was that Christianity should adapt itself to Asia's existing cultures. Had this directive been followed, a new epoch of world mission would have been inaugurated. Instead, with the outstanding exception of Jesuit Robert de Nobili, who addressed his ministry to high-caste Hindus and tried to express Catholic doctrine in a Hindu idiom, Latin Western forms of mission and church became the norm, despite the vast differences that distinguished the Indian situation from the one in which the Latin church itself had originated. The colonial churches and the missions later established by other missionaries from France, Italy, Spain and Germany unmistakably displayed the characteristics of these nations. The failure—and later official disapproval—of de Nobili's effort created a backlog of problems about the limits of inculturation that still deeply divide the Indian Catholic community.

The early 19th century soon exposed the Indian church to the consequences of Europe's changing balance of power. As the papacy became aware of Portugal's declining political leverage, it sought to supervise more closely India's Portuguese missions. The agency of this supervision was the Congregation for the Propagation of the Faith and the appointment of apostolic vicars. These vicars soon came into conflict with the local Portuguese clergy who, threatened with Roman authority, reasserted their traditional prerogatives, since it was, after all, the Portuguese Government that had appointed and supported the Catholic clergy in India. This conflict eventually permeated the whole Indian church and continued for much of the century. Although a preliminary agreement with Rome was reached in 1857, it was not until the new Concordat of 1886 that conflicting jurisdictions were resolved and an independent hierarchy was established for India and Ceylon (now Sri Lanka).

Thus, 1886 marked the beginning of a period of stabilization for the church. Admittedly, this stabilization retained much of the church's colonial character. The Indian church had its own hierarchy with clearly delineated ecclesiastical provinces headed by metropolitan sees. The autonomy of the Malabar and Malankara rites was formally recognized, although neither group received its own hierarchy until the first half of this century. A large group of native clergy emerged, and native seminaries were established. The school and hospital systems for which the Indian church was later to be so highly praised were consolidated as an integral part of the Church's mission. Numerous opportunities were created for non-Catholic Christians to participate with Catholics in evangelization. Although many of these took on competitive and political overtones in an effort to save the souls of "Indian pagans," they also led to beneficial results, such as education and health care for women. Finally, the church received its first Indian bishop.

With India's independence in 1947, Catholicism there redefined its objectives to fit more closely with the country's development goals. The Church's key concerns in the immediate pre-independence era were four: (1) establishing tighter bonds with other Christian groups in order to maintain the Catholic community's identity and autonomy in a predominantly Hindu culture; (2) safeguarding its right to evangelize through peaceful methods without detriment to the rights of the churches or of new converts; (3) protecting both the independence of Church-run institutions from government interference and the right of these institutions to qualify for government funding; and (4) articulating a rationale to justify "minority rights."

While these concerns also occupied the church's efforts for the first two decades after independence, a new priority has emerged since the early 1970s: redefining the task of evangelization to include the struggle for justice. This struggle acquired particular urgency as a growing number of Indians recognized that the country's growth strategy had not yielded sufficient benefits to meet either the needs of the marginalized classes or the population's rising expectations. Hence, some of the younger clergy vigorously urged that the church's principal concern should be the explicit promotion of justice, especially as the struggle for more economic benefits began to assume violent expression with the eruption of bloody clashes between different religious and caste groups. These clashes provided the context for India's state of emergency in 1975 and, almost a decade later, for the storming of the Sikhs' Golden Temple in Amritsar and the assassination of Indira Gandhi. In such circumstances, the Church was compelled to respond with a major effort at reconciling communal conflict.

At the same time, the Catholic Church experienced a dramatic increase in organizational size since independence. India today has more than 5,200 parishes, almost 90 percent of them with resident pastors; more than 17,000 missionary stations; and 125 bishops. The Catholic Bishops Conference of India was founded in 1945; India's First Plenary Council occurred in 1950. The major superiors of religious communities formed a national conference in 1960. There now exists an Indian Catholic Hospital Association and an All-India Catholic University Federation (for students), which was prefigured by the Congress of Catholic Universities in India begun in 1945.

> "*There are various challenges faced by Asian Indian immigrants. The greatest challenge for us, many of us feel, is to get accepted by the community at large without being forced to relinquish our own traditions, customs and value system.*"
> **An Indian priest**

Parallel to these organizational changes, the Church also underwent a qualitative growth and Indianization of its personnel, and continues a serious effort at cultural adaptation. India has an abundance of priestly and religious vocations—among the highest number anywhere in the world. Part of this growth results from the more than doubling of the Indian Catholic population over the last 30 years—from a little less than five million to almost 14 million today. Over the same 30-year period, the number of priests has trebled, from 3,500 to 12,000; religious sisters have quadrupled to about 50,000; religious brothers number almost 3,000; and seminarians number more than 8,000.

These growth patterns also revealed important regional differences. The new personnel were not always local. Most, in fact, came from the south and west of India. During the first decade after independence, a greater proportion of higher church offices were held by clergy from the west coast (Mangalore-Goa-Bombay), but slowly the balance has tilted in favor of the numerically strong and politically out-going southern groups. Today, more than 50 percent of all priests and 60 percent of all sisters come from Kerala. The same pattern is also noticeable in the appointment of bishops and major religious superiors.

In addition to the remarkable growth in church personnel since independence, there was a phenomenal increase in church-related institutions. In the past 30 years, university colleges have grown from 30 to more than 125 and their student population has increased by more than 1,000 percent (to over 145,000 today). High schools have increased from 30 to almost 3,000 and the number of high school students by more than 300 percent (to 1.7 million today). The number of primary schools is up to more than 6,200 and their students number above two million. Catholic hospitals have jumped from 53 to more than 600, dispensaries from 153 to over 1,500 and other charitable institutions such as leprosariums, orphanages and old age homes, have grown at similar rates. With the exception of primary schools, all these increases have been greatest in the last 20 years.

Besides an extraordinary vitality, these data also reflect some of the pastoral priorities of post-independence Catholicism. There has been a steady shift from evangelizing the Hindu heartlands of the north to increasing Catholic resources in the culturally more heterogeneous south, where Christianity has long had its strength. The growth in church-related institutions has been more of an urban than a rural phenomenon; 60 percent of it has occurred in towns of more than 100,000, while 70 percent of India's population lives in rural areas. The beneficiaries of the church services in the south are mostly the middle and lower classes. Those in the north come from the upper classes of the non-Christian majority; besides the families of government officials, these include politically important elements in state capitals and the new industrial bureaucrats of the public-sector townships that have appeared as a result of the country's planned development.

Challenges

These shifting priorities posed a number of complex challenges. In the years after independence, Catholicism in India became a fortress community, with the primary objective of safeguarding the rights of the church and improving its bargaining position in the larger society. This mentality, coupled with the spirituality prevalent in the pre-Vatican II period, ensured that the clergy remained primary in community affairs. The laity's minimal participation was reinforced by their own economic struggles, which left them little time for more active involvement. In the face of hardship, the marked Indian tendency toward inferiority acted as a palliative for their inability to change their material situation.

The need to energize the laity really has required transforming Indian Catholicism into an adult church. Here, the laity has been educated not only to understand the wider dimensions of their role as People of God, assuming fuller responsibility for the life of the Church, but also to complement their faith experience with a more active expression of "worldly" commitment, in which they perceive that the material efforts to move India into the 21st century constitute an important contribution to building up the Kingdom of God.

With this, the church's status as a minority religion in a vast non-Christian land has pointed to the need for increasing inter-religious dialogue with India's other major religions (Hinduism, Islam, and Buddhism), as well as the need to broaden the scope of Catholic evangelization. After 1947, the church became predominantly concerned with accumulating assets and institutions that would protect its existence. Today, both these strategies are under attack from social activists and mission workers who assert that evangelization must include the struggle for justice. The continuing coexistence of great poverty and misery amid great wealth gives such concerns pressing urgency. But the relation between social justice and evangelization has not been successfully articulated. Too often one encounters the tendency to reduce personal conversion to the struggle for justice, and vice versa.

Linked with the issue of evangelization, of course, has been the need to create an indigenous theology appropriate to today's Indian Church. While this need has been recognized throughout the subcontinent, the effort to create such an Indian theology has too often relied on an uncritical borrowing from Latin American liberation theology to establish a radical paradigm for social action. But India possesses its own spiritual resources that give it the ability to create an authentic Catholic theology based on indigenous conditions. Unlike liberation theology with its emphasis on "praxis," Indian religiosity is rooted in intense spiritual discipline emanating from the person who spends a whole lifetime reflecting on God. For the holistic traditions of India, the key value of any theology will be its focus on religious experience. A Catholic theology, moreover, will be authentically Indian to the extent that it is able to incorporate the twin conditions of poverty and religiosity. Efforts at inculturation will be successful under these same conditions.

Against this background, what can be said about the spiritual needs of Catholic Asian-Indian immigrants? Three issues seem paramount.

1. **Developing a "worldly" spirituality**. Asian-Indian Catholics come to the United States to escape material deprivation and make a good life for themselves and their families. Most of them become strong supporters of the American economic system and politically tend to be more conservative than liberal. A critical challenge facing these immigrants is how to reconcile their traditional practice of virtue (rooted in an experience of poverty and deprivation, a sense of fatalism, and a spiritual intensity that serves to compensate for what they cannot acquire elsewhere) with a spirituality of abundance. The issue here is not merely one of acculturation into the American ethos, but how to reconcile the love of God and God's call to witness to the Gospel in a situation where material goods are available without serious sacrifice. Immigration itself has removed one pillar on which their spirituality has rested.

What precisely is spirituality now in a situation of plenty? Poverty understood in the Indian tradition implies not only deprivation but also the attachment to illusion and greed. All the major Indian religions focus on the need for liberation from this illusion, which is defined as any activity that removes people from the ground of their being—Brahma or God. Within this context, a key value of any spirituality for Indian Catholic immigrants will be its recognition that material betterment is not an end in itself, but a means to greater interior freedom and union with God. At the same time, an absence of personal poverty does not mean the absence of social witness. The Asian Indian has a cultural penchant for self-absorption—a fierce concentration on one's own inner self, a desperate fight to hold on to one's idea of who he is, and a way of relating to the outside world principally in terms of how it affects the inner world of one's own feelings. This proclivity needs to be complemented by a more assertive orientation that perceives the world as a privileged place for actively witnessing to God's prophetic Word.

> "*We have to adopt the United States as our new home and reverse the attitude of some parish priests that still discriminate or do not accept the ethnic priests. The ethnic minority laity also has to be made more welcome and involved in the parish level so that they can feel that they belong.*"
> **An Indian parish minister**

2. **Maintaining a communal identity**. Asian-Indians bring with them a deep sense of religion which is expressed in a high level of sacramental practice, an intense religious discipline and interiority. Besides its profoundly personal dimension, Indian Catholic religiosity has also exhibited strong communal identification (centered in the family, the parish, and extending to the diocese). Hence, soon after their arrival in this country, most Asian-Indians search out and attach themselves to some local Catholic Indian group—most often a regional group (for example, from Goa, Mangalore, Kerala, Tamil Nadu, etc.) to replace the extended communities they left behind. The need to activate such communal (and familial) bonds is simply intensified by the small numbers of Asian-Indian Catholics both in India and in the United States. This situation thus poses a double challenge. The already widespread Indian practice of participating in the sacraments should be actively encouraged; at the same time, the need for communal identification with other Asian-Indians should be accommodated by encouraging both their own local associations and their participation in the institutional activities of their local parish and diocese. This participation would legitimize their own ethnic identification, while simultaneously integrating them into the way of being Catholic in America.

3. **Helping Asian-Indians to understand and take a part in the public role of Catholicism in American culture**. Catholics from India come from a church long marked by a singular obsession with making converts; Catholicism's more traditional missiology is deeply ingrained in their religious experience. In India, the church's vast web of institutions has been not only a protection for their

existence as a very small minority, but also clearly linked with both this missionary goal and the church's inter-religious dialogue. Coming to the United States, Asian-Indians find a different institutional structure with different missionary goals. They encounter a church with a long history of active involvement in public policy debates affecting the larger society. While these immigrants find living in a predominantly Christian culture extremely comfortable—no special effort is required, for example, to celebrate major Christian feasts such as Christmas and Easter when the whole culture celebrates them—they often have great difficulty in coming to grips with the social and political activism of American Catholicism. They are surprised by a church that takes public positions on issues—such as nuclear arms, the American economy, foreign aid, abortion and human rights—that are aimed not only at educating Catholics but at persuading the larger American society of the validity of the church's views and values.

Linking evangelization to the struggle for justice is even more recent in India than in the United States, and many Asian-Indian Catholics find it more difficult than American Catholics to articulate the relationship between them. This difficulty is rooted in the fact that the relationship between evangelization and the struggle for justice is basically straightforward in India: the presence of degrading poverty coupled with the inability of the state to mitigate it makes for an easy identification of the Catholic social mission. In the United States, Indian Catholics are not so exposed to such stark poverty; they know that, at least in theory, the state has the mechanisms to relieve it. As immigrants, they also possess a strong belief in self-reliance. In such circumstances, the Church's role in social justice, as well as the broader American definition of justice, is not so apparent.

Underneath all these issues, however, lies another and deeper question. Since independence, a persistent query facing Catholics in India has been how a person can be both authentically Indian and truly Catholic at the same time. With immigration, that question is transformed: How can Asian-Indians become truly American in a way that embodies both their Catholic and their cultural origins and that expresses an authentic Catholic commitment? Asian-Indians find themselves in a comfortable and generally welcoming religious environment that encourages their own personal and familial aspirations. They find it relatively easy to continue their previous attachment to Western forms of Catholicism in which they received their faith, but not so easy to deepen their religious commitment in a situation of comparative affluence. Further, American Catholicism itself is changing and these changes often directly challenge their accustomed ways of being Catholic. Meeting the needs of Asian-Indian Catholics is a manageable challenge, but it requires a special sensitivity to the historical and cultural context from which they come. It must be an exercise that looks forward as well as backward.

Footnotes

1. See Ronald Takaki, *Strangers From a Different Shore* (Boston: Little, Brown and Company, 1989), pp. 294-314. For more recent statistics and more attention to the religious factor, see Raymond Broody Williams, *Religions of Immigrants From India and Pakistan* (Cambridge and New York: Cambridge University Press), 1988.

2. For a fuller discussion of the history and changing situation of Asian-Indian Catholicism, see J. Walter Fernandes, SJ, "The Indian Catholic Community: A Minority in Search of Security," in *World Catholicism in Transition*, ed. Thomas M. Gannon, SJ (New York: Macmillan, 1988), pp. 362-378.

JAPAN

Japan is physically separated from the Asian continent by a relatively wide sea, the Sea of Japan and wide straits, both of which have enabled it to nurture an indigenous culture. A small country of 142,727 square miles, it is comprised of four main islands, Honshu, Kyushu, Shikoku and Hokkaido and many small islands. A territory smaller than that of California, consisting largely of rugged mountains, it is home to a population of 123 million people and ranks sixth in the size of countries.

Scholars point out that significant divisions within the East Asian countries are linguistic not racial. The written Japanese language is viewed as the most difficult language. Japanese is included in the Altaic languages, a division of the Sinitic linguistic family. Structurally it is quite different from Chinese but has borrowed many words from the Chinese language.

Japan's history dates back to 1500 BC and its recent history is characterized by two periods of swift modernization and adoption of western technology. At the present time it has one of the highest GNPs and is an economic force in the world of finance and business, while it maintains distinctly Japanese traditions and a national culture. This is the native country of the 800,000 Japanese Americans present in the United States today. Some of the historical trends, religious backgrounds, and the experience of Japanese people in America will be presented here with a particular emphasis on the role of religion.

Early History

The origins of Japanese history and culture are to be found in the Jomon stone age culture noted for its cord pattern pottery from the 4th and 5th centuries BC. From the following period of Yayoi culture during the 3rd century BC, its simple wheel-made pottery, the use of bronze and iron, and large earthen tumili erected over the tombs of leaders were developed.[1]

Two important Japanese records of early times compiled in the 1st century, Kojiki (Record of Ancient Matters) and Nihon Shoki Nihonji (History of Japan) began with myths. They centered around a divine brother and sister who created the islands of Japan, and the presence of several deities including Amaterasu, the sun goddess. Her grandson Ninigi came to earth bringing with him the three imperial regalia which remain today as the symbols of imperial authority. These are the bronze mirror (the symbol of Amaterasu), the iron sword, and the necklace of "curved jewels". Ninigi established the Japanese state on the Yamato plain and became the first emperor Jimmu (Divine Warrior) in 660 BC.

Throughout the 1st century, Japanese society was divided into a large number of family or family-related groups each called an "uji" under a chief, and worshipping an uji god, usually an ancestor. Hence there was no real line between religion and government at this time.

Between the 5th and 8th century Japan developed a high degree of cultural sophistication. During the Taika period, begun in 645, Chinese culture and Chinese models were incorporated.

Buddhism was introduced to Japan during the 5th century through Korea when the Korean state of Paekche presented an image of Buddha and scriptures to the Yamato court and it became the conduit for Chinese culture. Prince Shotoku (574-622) promoted reverence for Buddhism and for Confucian virtues. He established a centralized bureaucracy of government, adopted the Chinese calendar, and sent many ambassadors to China. This was the epitome of Chinese political power in Japan. However, the system which eventually evolved was one quite different from the Chinese.

Under the Emperor Tenchi and his successors, a permanent capital was established in Heijo (Nara). Even today the imperial family follows the sacerdotal role of the early sun line uji of Yamato.

During the following Heian Period (794-1185), the capital moved to Kyoto, where it remained until 1865 and the Meiji Restoration. From a highly centralized government, Japan moved to a more native style of governance based on familial and personalized relations. Each group was responsible only to the group immediately above it. Economic and political power was held through noble families and strong religious institutions (Buddhist temples and Shinto shrines) rather than through a centralized government.

> "*I* am a Japanese American. I am also a Catholic. During the World War II Japanese American internment, the Church as a whole (as an institutional and hierarchical body) did not show a policy or any sensitivity toward the idea of human rights. We, as Japanese Americans and as Catholics, were stripped of our basic human rights. Yet, the Church to which I belong did not even respond."
>
> **A Japanese educator**

One of these families, the Fujiwara family had almost complete control of the emperor's family providing empresses and imperial concubines. Four emperors married the daughters of Michinaga, the most famous of the Fujiwara regents. Though wielding great power, they never moved to usurp the throne. Respect for hereditary power and the religious role of the imperial family was strong. It was a time of great growth, economically and culturally. New efforts were made to imitate Chinese culture; consequently, Chinese culture was absorbed into the native culture thus forming the pattern for all subsequent Japanese civilization.

Buddhism became Japanese in that rather than being a religion of the aristocracy it related to the common people. Art forms used basic Chinese forms expressed in essentially Japanese ways, e.g., Yamatoe, a style of simple flowing lines and flat colored spaces.

Feudalism

Beginning in the 9th century, provincial authorities found it necessary to protect themselves against armed bandits by organizing local family-based bands led by members of the local aristocracy. The local warrior aristocracy which emerged had become prominent by the 12th century and was called the bushi (warrior) or samurai (retainer). It was a social and political structure similar to the later feudal system in Europe. Continuing into the following Kamakura period (1189-1336) under the leadership of the Yoritomo family, a stable period of peace and order prevailed.

Domestic and international commerce grew rapidly at the same time that these feudal structures flourished. Political power became centralized in the late 16th century through a feudal system of daimyo domains. The feudal system which arose had characteristics which were quite different from the system which arose in Europe. With this familial institution as a base, there developed a national culture and ethnic uniformity, as well as a strong tradition of and acceptance of national unity. Japan's centralized feudalism has been described as almost a contradiction from the point of view of the European feudal experience in Europe.

Feudalism in Japan had three stages: 1) the single lord-vassal band of the Kamakura period; 2) multiple lord-vassal groups of the Ashikaga period; and 3) the centralized political power through the Daimyo during the Tokugawa period. The feudal system provided Japan for almost three centuries with unusual stability characterized by an "efficiency in political administration and economic integration not seen anywhere in Europe before the 19th century."[2]

This period witnessed the arrival of the Portuguese in 1543 and of St. Francis Xavier in 1549, both bringing Christian missionaries. While at first Japanese saw Christianity as a variation of popular Buddhism, this changed when the daimyo in Kyushu became Christian, and was followed by the people in their domain. The small Omura daimyo founded the port of Nagasaki for Portuguese trade in 1562, and actually assigned its control to the Jesuits. Thus Catholicism grew rapidly in Kyushu and also in the Kyoto area.[3] It is estimated that the Catholic population there was as high as half a million in 1615. Eventually tensions arose between allegiance to Japan and to a distant alien pope. This led to Christianity's being seen as subversive, and persecutions followed.

Persecution and Freedom of Religion

During the feudal period of the Tokugawas, Tokugawa Ieyasu first allowed the Spanish Franciscans to establish a mission in Edo (Tokyo), but later issued anti-Christian decrees. His successor, Tokugawa Hidetada banned all Christian missionary activity, and persecution became widespread. The revolt of the largely Christian peasants in Shimabara against excessive taxation led to Japan's almost complete isolation from the outside world for two centuries.

Following the Meiji Restoration, the new constitution of 1890 established freedom of religion. However, with increasing nationalism during and after World War II, State Shintoism became dominant. Christianity, seen as a "foreign" religion, came under great suspicion and a central Japanese Christian Church was established. However, with the promulgation of a new constitution in 1947, freedom of religion was and still is allowed.

Japanese Traditional Folk Religion

When one thinks of Japanese religion, commonly Buddhism and Shintoism are mentioned. However, the religion of Japan which is most fundamentally Japanese is an immanent folk religion.

In a discussion on Japanese religion, Munakata writes that ultimate concerns are those that involve humankind most profoundly. The term is usually considered synonymous with "God". The eighteenth-century Shinto thinker Moto'ori Norinaga, writing in his Kojikiden (Commentary on the Kojiki), defines god or the kami as having three natures: "It is extraordinary. It is exceedingly virtuous. It is greatly fearsome." Moto'ori deemed that humankind's finite knowledge and wisdom could never totally know the true nature of the kami. A God has the power not only to provoke fear and trembling in human beings, but also to seduce them with love and stir their souls.

A Catholic and a sociologist of religion, Munakata conceptualizes the characteristics of the religious beliefs that form the central axis of a culture formed in the "historical body" called Japan. One must not forget to include the influence of Buddhism, Confucianism, and Christianity, all of which were added to and absorbed into the original folk religion. The focus of this discussion is the realm of indigenous Japanese religion.[4]

An Immanentist Religious Culture

The basic characteristic of Japanese folk religion can be referred to as an "immanentist religious culture." This contrasts with the basic characteristic of Western Christianity, which is that of a "transcendentalist religious culture." Similar immanentist religious cultures are found throughout the countries of Asia. Japanese folk religion represents only one variant among a large category of immanentist religions.

The immanentist world is based on religious sentiments that developed in the natural setting and climate of Japan and in the daily experiences of the communal village life of farming and fishing. In particular it is characterized by ancestor worship and nature worship. It contrasts with, for example, Christ and the self-revelation of a transcendent god, for immanentist religious culture is based on religious sentiments evoked by humans living in a natural environment. Ultimate concerns are represented by the *kami* who are believed to be immanent in this world.

In a transcendental religious culture, as in the case of Christianity, this world and its inhabitants are the creation of a transcendent God, with humankind and God bound together in a bond of love. The purpose of this world lies ultimately in serving the greater glory of this God, and the natural world is therefore thought of as an object to be used and controlled by humans.

According to the sentiments of immanentist religion, although the gods reside in the world of souls, they have ready access to this world and are therefore immanent. According to surveys conducted in traditional Japanese farming village communities, daily labor, family living, and village activity are not merely activities involving the use of instruments. Instead, they are activities of deep religious meaning. In these villages, there are rituals, festivals, and religious objects that represent the immanent gods' continual intercourse with village life. Indeed, the rites of ancestor and nature worship are symbolic ceremonies giving concrete imagery to this intercourse. In a passage concerning the welcoming of the souls of the dead at the Bon festivals held throughout Japan in the summer, Yanagita Kunio says in "Senzo no hanashi" (About our ancestors) that beliefs in an immanentist religious culture are learned gradually through a long, experiential process—or in his words, through "unconscious transmission".[5] Consequently, such beliefs do not exist in the form of logically organized dogma. They are sentiments that enrich and give meaning to the totality of life.

> "*I* became a Catholic when I was 16. It went against my father's wish. 'Over my dead body,' he said. I'm falling away from the church and many of the people I know stop going to church. They go to the Protestant church because of the fellowship."
>
> **A Japanese woman**

In an immanentist religious world, nature possesses a symbolic meaning that reinforces the folk religion. The believer projects his religious faith onto the natural environment. Yanagita cites Sai-no-kahara on Tobishima Island, Sado, Niigata Prefecture, as a natural setting which the Japanese have endowed with religious meaning.[6]

According to the oral legends of the islanders, the rocks that surround a great cliff that stands in the ocean opposite Sai-no-kahara have meaning as "the stepping stones to the other world" for the souls of the dead. Endowing nature with meaning is the characteristic of an immanentist religious culture. The same basic religious sentiments are also observable in the worship of yama no kami ("kami of the mountain") and ta no kami ("kami of the rice field") in farming villages and in the worship of umi no kami ("kami of the sea") among fishing villagers or inhabitants of remote islands.

The Afterworld in the World

Parallelism is another characteristic of immanentist religious cultures. This is a religious faith that depicts the life of the soul in the afterworld in terms of the basic patterns of life in this world. The afterworld takes this world as its standard. For example, the path to adulthood is celebrated on the following ritual occasions: the seventh day after birth (shichiya); a shrine visit thirty or thirty-one days after birth; kuizome or "first food" on the hundredth day after birth (rice is prepared and fed to the baby in symbolic representation of its having been weaned; in actuality, however, the family only goes through the motions of feeding the child—who will not be weaned for some time); visits to the shrine at ages three, five, and seven (shichi-go-san); and marriage.

The soul of the deceased is honored on the seventh, thirty-ninth, and hundredth days after passing on to the other world, and rites are observed in the following years after death: 1, 3, 7, 13, 17, 23, 33, and 50. After the fiftieth year, the individual soul is considered to have merged with the realm of the spirits.

Harmony With Nature

Japanese immanentist religious culture can be looked at in terms of our relationship to nature: our subjugation to nature, our harmony with nature, and our mastery over nature. Japanese culture belongs to the second category. In this category there is no real separation between us, nature, and the supernatural. "One is simply an extension of the other, and a concept of wholeness derives from their unity. We are in harmony with nature."

This characteristic is also observable in Shinto thinking. Shintoists believe in the immortality of the soul and posit the existence of two realms, one for the living and one for the dead. To describe the latter they use many words, for example, takamagahara ("the heavenly fields"), tokoyo no kuni ("the world beyond"), yomi no kuni ("the land of darkness"), and kakuriyo ("the hidden realm"). They do not, however, think of this realm as a heaven or utopia in an afterlife that is divorced from this world. The worlds of the living and the dead are enveloped within the one immanentist religious realm. Consequently, at either thirty-three or fifty years after death, the souls of the dead come together and merge into one great body of souls. Before undergoing this unification, they make frequent visits to the world of the living. The souls of the ancestors return to the homes of their descendants every year at specified periods or on special occasions when ceremonies are performed to call them back.

A number of symbolic rituals are carried out in the family house in order to receive the visiting soul. In advance of the Bon Festival of the Dead held according to the traditional calendar on July 13th, food is specially prepared, the house and its furnishings are given a thorough cleaning and polishing, and new wardrobes are made ready. The normal work routine is suspended, and the children are reminded to be on their best behavior. In some farming villages, the farmers will not scythe in the fields for fear of injuring the feet of their ancestors as they make their way across for the return home.[7] The Japanese feel a closeness and intimacy with the world of the dead because:

    1) Even though a person has died, the soul continues to reside in Japan and does not go far away;

    2) There is constant contact between this and the other world and the dead return not just at the time of the annual festivals, but can, at the instigation of either party, be recalled to the world of the living without difficulty;

    3) The wishes one expresses on one's deathbed will inevitably be fulfilled;

    4) The dead not only establish plans on behalf of their descendants but also, by being reborn into a second and third life, actively work to carry them out.[8]

Belief in rebirth found among Japanese differs from the Buddhist idea of the transmigration of the soul. The belief concerning the two realms of the living and the dead is a synthesis of the images of this dedication to the well-being of one's community and family—the pillars of an immanentist religion. In addition, evil is looked on as the work of the gods of the "world of darkness".[9] Calamity and ill-fortune are avoided by the performance of rituals like misogi (purification by water) and harae (purification by the waving of holy objects).

Shinto

Shinto admits of none of the Christian ideas of sin, atonement, and divine forgiveness. In Shinto the word matsuri (festival) has an all-important meaning. A matsuri is a religious ceremony held in order to commune with the gods; matsurigoto (which once meant administrative action but now means festive acts) are performed on behalf of the gods to assure prosperity. In order to perform matsurigoto or festival roles, properly, the rites of purification cited above are performed. Formal Shinto thought thus consists of a systematized, "ideologized" version of the nature-centered religious values of the indigeneous folk religion. In this sense the political ideology of national Shinto has evolved from a prototype immanentist religious culture found in the daily life of the Japanese people and in the beliefs they have transmitted across the ages.

Modernization and Immanentist Religion

A discussion of the effect of modernization on the kind of traditional immanentist religion seen in Japanese society raises a number of important problems. In particular, what occurred when basic changes in the social structure resulting from modernization had penetrated into the daily life of the Japanese?

Ancestor and nature worship formed the basis of Japanese religious life, and these beliefs naturally grew out of and were fostered in the farming, fishing, and mountain villages scattered throughout the "monsoon-type climate". Folk beliefs changed in the course of modernization and we shall try to identify the types of religious social character that emerged.

We have referred to the traditional religious culture of Japan as immanentist. Consequently, we may think of the corresponding religious social character as immanentist. The immanentist believer holds that the gods dwell in this world so the worship of ancestors and nature is fostered. Such a person practices a lifestyle based on the religious values inherent in such forms of worship. This type of believer perceives the divine in the midst of nature, refuses to treat natural objects purely as instruments, and feels that contact with nature involves latently religious meaning. In the social environment, kinship bonds and ties to the land are strong, and human relations and organization are heavily imbued with religious meaning. In a self-sufficient culture, persons will learn their society's religious sentiments unconsciously, and their commitment to their faith is often stronger than the faith of one who has acquired their beliefs through the formal study of dogma or an intellectual decision.

Though the immanentist type is representative of a highly provincial culture, it is not necessarily intolerant of foreign cultures or religions. So long as the basic beliefs of the religious community remain unscathed, the community will be open to outside beliefs.

The second type of religious social character is the latent immanentist type, product of a latent-immanentist religious culture. Though social behavior is conducted along the rational lines inherent in industrial society, nevertheless traditional religious values continue to operate on a latent level. Culturally speaking, these people possess a dual social character. Because the internalization of traditional values occurred spontaneously and naturally during childhood, they are often retained on an unconscious level into adulthood.

A study of Catholic parishioners revealed that the ideas parishioners held concerning life after death showed the same traditional immanentist religious world view that Yanagita described in "About our Ancestors". For example, in response to the question "Where do you think your ancestors are?" —a question that relates to an immanentist point of view—only 3 out of the 100 interviewees replied tengoku or "heaven" (in the sense posited by Catholicism). The interviewees were people who lived in the midst of urban culture, were steady churchgoers who, despite their heavy exposure to Catholic doctrine, displayed the classical immanentist religiosity of traditional Japanese religious culture. Although the vast majority of middle-aged Japanese live outwardly according to patterns of contemporary urban behavior, it would appear that they still retain a traditional immanentist orientation in their deeply internalized religious sentiments. Despite the high degree of technological sophistication, the existence of life employment and seniority systems in Japanese industrial organizations is indicative of how deeply rooted Japanese traditions are in the area of human relationships.

The perpetuation of these deeply rooted, latent immanentist religious values is reflected in the process by which Christianity has been diffused in Japan. It is evident, for example, in the remark by the Christian author Masamune Hakucho (1879-1962) who describes Christianity as "a harsh religion denying this world" or in Endo Shusaku's novel *Chinmoku (Silence)* which takes as its theme the role of Christianity in Japan. One of the novel's central characters, the Catholic priest Ferreira, states that Japanese culture rejects Christianity: "It is a swamp that rots the roots of Christianity." Again, "The Japanese are not able to think of God completely divorced from man.... The Japanese imagine a beautiful, exalted man, and this they call God."

Endo's novel evoked considerable debate within Christian circles in Japan, but more important, he created in his novel the atmosphere of traditional Japanese immanentist religious culture. Though *Chinmoku* is written in the form of a historical novel, it addresses itself to the problem inherent in an encounter between Japanese culture, which is strongly immanentist, and Western Christianity, which is transcendental in nature.

The third type of religious social character is the "post-immanentist" type. It is the product of changes in the external social environment such as urbanization and industrialization, as well as the cessation of the socialization process which in the past transmitted traditional religious values. Living in a rapidly changing social environment, many parents have lost the confidence to preserve the traditional way of life they once learned and therefore do not pass it on to their children.

As a result of the disintegration of the essential social, cultural, and physical conditions required to sustain traditional beliefs, the traditional Japanese value system has tended to disappear heteronomously, that is, because of external authority and hierarchical laws and influence. This has created a momentary and partial vacuum in Japanese religious culture.

Though the secularized industrial society of modern Japan may be able to bequeath technological roles to its youth, it seems unable to equip its young people with a religious culture. Some youths long nostalgically for this now lost traditional world and engage in sentimental fantasies about its restoration. But the general trend is for young people to have little empathy for the traditional religious world. The results of a survey on "The youth of the world and the youth of Japan" released in July, 1973 support this conjecture. This survey was conducted among youths aged 18 to 22 in ten countries, each sample group consisting of 2,000 persons.[10] It suggests that Japanese youth have largely abandoned their traditional immanentist religious culture even on the latent level and that in comparison with the youth of other nations they are extremely dissatisfied with their lives in a rapidly expanding industrial civilization.

Buddhism, Confucianism, and Christianity are, in this system, relegated to positions on the periphery of this native religious culture. These foreign religions may have influenced the native culture to some extent, but they were also transformed by it. Historically speaking, one can say that although Japanese religious culture has been influenced by foreign religions, the religious beliefs that constitute the core of the uniquely Japanese culture have not disintegrated. The changes, however, that modernization has produced in the basic structure of Japanese society do, as stated above, threaten the continued existence of this basic core. Modernization represents a serious crisis for traditional Japanese folk religion.

The Catholic Church in Japan Today

More than a century has passed since the ban against Christian religions was lifted by the Meiji government. Christians altogether are less than one percent of the population; Protestants number around 600,000 and Catholics about 400,000.

Table 1: Japanese Catholics

1900	55,091
1920	76,404
1940	119,224
1960	277,502
1980	406,796
1985	432,857

Source: *World Catholicism in Transition*.[11]

The period following the end of World War II was the period of highest growth in the number of Catholics. Since then the number has grown by about 5,000 annually. The influence of Catholicism is mediated through its various schools, social welfare and other institutions. However, for most Japanese, Christianity is intrinsically linked to Western culture, and is therefore perceived as an international religious institution.

There are two basic groups of Japanese Catholics. First, the descendants of the Nagasaki Christians inherited a Catholicism born out of persecution. They are socially conservative, uphold traditional doctrines, and reside in closely knit lower-class communities. The second group consists of new converts and their families who are usually from the main cities, the urban middle-class, and are generally open to change.

At the turn of the century and through 1960, the Nagasaki dioceses had almost twice as many Catholics as the city of Nagasaki, where Catholicism began much earlier in Japan.

Among Asian countries, Japan has the highest ratio of pastoral workers to laity. Japan has seen a large number of vocations to the priesthood and more especially to orders of women religious of whom the majority, 90%, are Japanese. Among priests, the proportion of Japanese and foreign clergy is about equal. Since the beginning of World War II, all bishops have been Japanese and the Japanization of central administration of the Church has progressed rapidly. However, the presence of foreign priests and religious remains a strong influence and plays a prominent role in the Catholic Church in Japan.

Even though there has been a diminishment of foreign religious presence, it has not produced an inculturation of Catholicism. As a result, the role of the laity has been difficult, because Japanese society is male-dominated. Nevertheless, in evangelizing and serving as catechists, the laity has always undertaken responsibility and initiatives.

In Japanese culture, a weekly religious observance does not exist, therefore, many Japanese Catholics do not perceive Mass as a strict obligation. Catholics remain faithful to the church and are members of a parish, but other forces mitigate against a regular Sunday attendance. For many women a regular weekly attendance is especially difficult, since they are expected to stay home on weekends when their husbands and children are at home. Most Catholics celebrate a church wedding, but three-quarters are mixed marriages between a Christian and non-Christian.

Nevertheless, "church weddings" have become desirable for non-Christian couples, where they have been welcomed by the church as occasions for evangelization. A special service has been authorized by the Japanese bishops for this occasion.

The Japanese Church has joined the Federation of Asian Bishops Conference in responding to needs in Asia. Especially, the Japanese Church responded generously to the refugee problem at the end of the Vietnamese War, setting an example of involvement in Asian social issues. Japanese missionaries abroad, especially women religious, and the Japanese Council for Justice and Peace have contributed to the vitality of Catholicism in Japan.

The development of Catholicism is viewed in two ways. First, it has the appeal of a universal religion with an international structure which Japanese see as related to the growth of the nation as a global economic power. On the other hand, the universality of the church is viewed as a serious barrier to other schools of religion from the point of view of Catholic authors such as Shusako Endo and Peter Munakata. They seek the expression of their faith in the depths of their being Japanese and in an understanding of the immanent characteristics of traditional religion integral to Japan. Perhaps the incarnational theology of God's presence found in the theology of the Second Vatican Council might bring to the Japanese the presence of our God and the Christian spirit. Indeed, our faith would be made all the richer in this mutual searching for God who is both immanent and transcendent.

Sojourn to the United States

Strangers From A Different Shore is the first and only social history to document in careful historical and experiential narrative the arrival and hopes of many immigrants from Asia to the United States. The author, Ronald Takaki, is an American of Japanese descent whose grandparents came to the United States around the turn of the century, and whose parents were agricultural entrepreneurs on the west coast. Another active Catholic lay leader speaks of his grandfather who came to Hawaii from Japan and was a Shinto priest, and of his father who labored on the plantations in Hawaii. Both bring to us a fairly typical picture of the arrival of Japanese immigrants to these shores.

Following the arrival of Commodore Perry to Japan in 1853 after almost two centuries of isolation, a ban on emmigration was continued until 1884. Recruitment of small numbers of Japanese laborers to Hawaii, and to a silk farm in California took place surreptitiously. In the 1880s Japanese immigrants began coming to Hawaii and in the 1890s to the U.S. mainland in significant numbers. They were persuaded to emigrate both by the economic situation in their homeland and the active contract labor program especially from Hawaii. They came with the determination to migrate, work hard, send money back, and to return to Japan to regain the land they had lost and pay family debts.[12]

Between 1885 and 1924, 200,000 Japanese went to Hawaii and 180,000 to the mainland. This emigration was a carefully planned one. They were a select group carefully screened by the government to be healthy, literate, and uphold national honor. Initially they were only men, but women were later also persuaded to emigrate. Some came through arranged marriages, others were workers following the pattern already established in Japan, where women in the 19th century were wage-earners in such industries as tea processing and paper making.

With the annexation of Hawaii in 1900, contract labor was prohibited and the 1908 Gentleman's Agreement restricted Japanese immigration except for immediate family members. Long term emigration then became the more desirable pattern.

In the 1920s anti-Japanese hostility was present in the United States. However, the situations in Hawaii and on the mainland were very different. In Hawaii, most people were Asian, of which the Japanese comprised 43%, and the labor market was particularly dependent on Japanese and Filipino workers. A combination of unionization, politics and collective action was the strategy used to deal with the labor problems. In contrast, on the West coast, Asians were few although Japanese were the largest group. With the campaigns to keep them out of the California labor market, Japanese rallied around ethnic solidarity and ethnic enterprise and became small shopkeepers and small farmers. They developed a separate and very successful Japanese economy and community as a defense against social exclusiveness. Takaki goes on to point out that "their very withdrawal into these self-contained communites for survival and protection reinforced claims of their unassimilability and their condition as 'strangers.'"

From 4,700 acres in 1900, Japanese Americans in California owned almost half a million acres of land by 1920. In 1882, Japanese Americans numbered 2,030; twenty years later, they were almost 150,000 mostly on the Pacific coast. They converted marginal lands in the Sacramento and Imperial Valleys into productive farmlands and built an immigrant economy on Japanese ethnic solidarity and mutual support systems developed in the United States. These support systems reflect mutual cooperation which is deeply rooted in Japanese culture.

Many of the laws passed during the early 1900s were aimed at curtailing immigration and restricting the economic leadership. These restricted the length of terms of lease for agricultural lands, the right to naturalization, and the entry of aliens ineligible for citizenship. So, for their American-born children they stressed hard work and education to overcome the handicap of discrimination.

Later, this discrimination was to lead to the organization of the young Japanese Americans around the Japanese American Citizen League as *nisei* (second generation) sought to become "one hundred percent American."

The height of discrimination occurred during World War II when Japanese Americans, including those who were U.S. citizens, were put into internment camps. Even following the closing of these camps, prejudice continued with the policy to resettle Japanese in dispersed sites. One consequence of this was that the Japanese American Catholic community has been scattered. Maryknoll parishes, for example, which had formed the core of such communities, were suppressed by Catholic bishops to discourage the coming together of a Japanese community and to hasten assimilation. While appreciating the support of individual priests, many regret the lack of support from church structures.

At the present time the Catholic community continues to be a scattered community and a particular challenge to the church. In addition to the immigrant experience out of which the Japanese American has struggled with great dignity, as demonstrated by their senators and scholars, it is important to understand something of the historical and cultural roots out of which so much of their important values and principles came.

Footnotes

1. John K. Fairbanks, Edwin O. Reischauer and Albert M. Craig, *East Asia, Tradition and Transformation*, Rev. ed., Boston, Houghton Mifflin Co., 1989, p.2. (Historical data are from this publication.)

2. *Ibid.*, p. 393.

3. *Ibid.*, p. 393-4.

4. Iwao Munakata, "Ambivalent Effects of Modernization on Traditional Folk Religion," *Japanese Journal of Religious Studies*, Vol. 3, No. 2-3, June-September, 1976. (Traditional Religion sections are excerpted from this paper.)

5. Kunio Yanagita, "Tamashii no Yukue" ("Whither Our Souls?"), in *Senzo no Hanashi (About Our Ancestors): Collected Works of Kunio Yanagita*, Vol. 10 and Vol. 15, 1962, pp. 108-110.

6. *Ibid.*, p. 128.

7. *Ibid.*, p. 110.

8. *Ibid.*, p. 120.

9. Sokyo Ono, "Matsuri Shinto", ("Shinto Festivals"), in *Dialogue on Religion: Christianity and Other Religions of Japan*, Tokyo, Sobunsha, 1973, p. 51-75.

10. Sorifu Seishonen Taisuku Honba, (Head Office of the Prime Minister's Committee on Youth), *Sekai no Seinento Nihon no Seinen, (The Youth of the World and the Youth of Japan)*, 1973.

11. Jan Swyndgedouw, "The Awakening of a Local Church: Japanese Catholicism in Tension Between Particularistic and Universal Values," in *World Catholicism in Transition*, edited by Thomas M. Gannon, SJ, New York, Macmillan Publishing Co., 1988, p. 380.

12. Ronald Takaki, *Strangers From A Different Shore*, Boston, Little, Brown and Company, 1989. (The section on Sojourn of Japanese to the U.S. is based on this documentation of Asian immigrant history.)

KOREA

The Beginning

Around the third millennium B.C., tribal people from the Altaic Mountains began migrating eastward to Manchuria and Siberia. Some of them, believed to be Tungusic in origin, went as far as the coasts of the Korean peninsula. These people loved what they saw and began to make their homes there. Eventually they became a homogeneous race sharing distinct physical characteristics, one language and one culture. Today they are known as the Korean people.[1]

The History

As the people who settled on the Korean peninsula began to form different family groups, many clans emerged. Some clans dominated other clans. The Ancient Choson was the first of these. The legendary founder was Tan-gun, the mythical progenitor of the Korean people, who welded the various tribes into a single kingdom. His era lasted more than 1,200 years. About a century after his era, the Ancient Choson split into various communities. In 109 B.C., the remnants of the Ancient Choson in the north were taken over by the Han Empire of China.[2]

Three centuries later, when China lost dominance in the area, the three kingdoms of Koguryo, Paekche and Shilla emerged. The influences of Buddhism and Confucianism also came into play, as is apparent in the state codes and in the hierarchical structures, with the king at the pinnacle. Toward the eighth century, Shilla, the last to achieve statehood, through the leadership of General Kim Yu-shin, led an attack against China. His goal: to take the Korean Peninsula and unite the people of the three kingdoms. He succeeded, and thus was born the Unified Shilla (668-935).[3]

During this era, Buddhism became the state's greatest influence, seen in attempts to establish the ideal Buddhist state and state Buddhist temple. Buddhist scriptures were being printed at this time. The economy was good and people enjoyed an affluent life. The capital city was also alive and vibrant.

However, the Unified Shilla did not enjoy its prosperity for long. In the ninth century the kingdom was shaken by intra-clan conflicts and the disturbances from the district administration. The rebel leader, Wang Kon, supported by landlords and merchants, led an uprising and enthroned himself as the founder king of Koryo.[4] He legitimized his rule by marrying into the Shilla royal clan. The Koryo

38

kingdom (918-1392) was thus established.

Milestones in this era included the emancipation of slaves by King Kwangjong (949-975). The government was restructured into a system that empowered the officials to admonish the throne and to censor royal decisions. Confucianism also was becoming a major influence. Around the mid-12th century, the world's first known moveable metal typography and bronze coin casting technology were invented here.[5]

Despite these developments, the kingdom was often undermined by internal conflicts which eventually yielded to a new dynasty. General Yi Song-gye, who realized that the Koryo monarchy was in decline, set out to restore the kingdom. After gaining power by driving out Japanese pirates, he established the Choson kingdom (1392-1910).[6] During this monarchy, Confucian humanism received its greatest attention under King Sejong the Great (1418-1450). He measured and evaluated official rulers through the Confucian tradition. During his reign, progressive ideas flourished. His administration was noted for restructuring linguistics, science, music, medical science and humanistic studies. He showed concern for the farmers by establishing drought and flood relief. However, his most important contribution, in 1446, was the creation of the Korean alphabet, han-gul, which was the script for vernacular language.[7]

During the Choson kingdom, there arose many conflicts from all sides. External pressure came from the Japanese empire, which made its presence felt around the regions. The Japanese invasion in the late 1500s left Korean land and its people devastated. In China, the Ming dynasty came into power but also was crushed by Japanese invasions.[8]

> "*We need to hear more candidly from our Pacific Rim people exactly what needs they are experiencing so that we can meet those needs. We are more ready to hear their needs than to say how we will respond to those needs.*"
>
> **A priest ministering with the Asian community**

In the early 17th century, Korean scholars continued to enjoy the atmosphere of learning in pragmatic studies. They studied solutions to the social problems through administrative reforms in land distribution and agricultural improvements. Western technologies were gradually introduced and adopted. The development during the 17th and 18th centuries in some respects resembled the Western European Renaissance.[9] During this time, the kingdom improved its economic and social situations.

During the late 19th century, Korea was forced to open to the outside world. England, Russia, Prussia, other European nations, and the United States made demands upon the Korean government to open commercial relations, at times resorting to military power. Meanwhile, Japan eyed these events with interest. The Japanese government attacked Chinese warships on July 25, 1894 near Asan Bay along the west coast. Thus began the Sino-Japanese War, in which the Chinese lost nearly all the battles. During the course of the war, the Japanese forced Korea to implement reforms that included hiring Japanese military instructors to train Korean military officers who were assigned to the royal palace. Korea's Queen Min made secret overtures to China and Russia. Upon discovering Queen Min's intention, the Japanese assassinated her on October 8, 1895. The history of outright Japanese control in Korea began with the establishment of the Residency General on February 1, 1906. In the summer of 1910, an agreement on Korea-Japan Annexation was signed and immediately went into effect, on August 22. The Choson kingdom came to an end.[10]

While under Japanese rule, many Koreans struggled internally to free themselves from the Japanese colonialists. March 1, 1919 marked an important day for the Koreans. A Declaration of Independence was drawn up by 33 leaders of the freedom movement.[11] Though the Japanese reacted swiftly with violence against the freedom movement and its people, the resistance gained momentum and received support from people in all walks of life. Japanese oppression in Korea included the suppression of Koreans' freedom of religion; banning Korean language classes from primary and secondary school; and a massive forced mobilization of Korean manpower and materials into Japan's World War II efforts.

When the Japanese government surrendered to the Allies on August 15, 1945, Korea gained its independence from Japan. However, the joy of liberation was short-lived, as Korea immediately faced other ordeals. The Korean people found themselves in a partitioned nation, the victims of ideological conflicts that surfaced after four decades of Japanese domination. Korea was divided on the 38th parallel and placed under the trusteeship of four nations: the U.S., the U.S.S.R., Britain, and China.[12] A communist government was imposed in the north and the Republic of Korea, a democracy, was established in the south. The new southern government faced the pressing task of rebuilding its own nation once again.

Rebuilding was difficult for the Republic of Korea, but the people were determined to make it work. In the midst of rebuilding, South Koreans found themselves at war one morning in June 1950.[13] Without warning, North Korean troops crossed the 38th parallel and swept down upon the unprepared south. The Republic of Korea appealed to the United Nations. The Security Council responded by passing the resolution demanding that communist North Korea withdraw its troops; the Council also encouraged the member nations to give military support. The battles were fierce and claimed many casualties in the three-year war (South Korean troops, 147,000; U.N. troops, 35,000; North Korean troops, 520,000; Red Chinese soldiers, 900,000; non-military casualties in South Korea, 245,000).[14] The war finally reached a stalemate and the Russians called for a truce negotiation in July 1951. The cease fire agreement was finally reached in July 1953.

Once again, the Republic of Korea faced the task of rebuilding. After the Korean war the country was in search of the best political system to serve its people. It succeeded in setting up the Military Revolution Committee in May, 1961. This Committee changed its name to the Supreme Council for National Reconstruction and gradually made arrangements to restore civilian rule.[15] Under the Third, Fourth and Fifth Republics, Korea grew into a powerful economic force. Today Korea has finally approached the status from which she can be influential in the international community.

Korean Religions, People, Ideas and Values

Buddhism, Confucianism and Animism have been major influences on Korean ideas and values. Buddhism teaches that people can break the endless human cycle of good and evil by choosing an alternative lifestyle—a path that transcends the grip of evil and reorients the individual's life towards good. Through this alternative lifestyle, the Buddhist seeks to reach the ultimate state of goodness, which is called nirvana. Compassion, gentleness and kindness are considered as the practical way to nirvana. The Buddhist ideal of compassion, morality, unity and harmony with all creation has contributed much to Asian culture; Korea is no exception.[16] Buddhism entered Korea via Chinese and Indian missionaries around 372. It was accepted as a state religion for some time, after the initial rejection by the Shilla government. The type of Buddhism which entered Korea was the Mahayana, the "greater vehicle." Mahayana Buddhism is more liberal than Theravada Buddhism. It is a humane and magnanimous religion which makes concessions to popular piety. In Mahayana Buddhism, Bodhisattva, the one destined for enlightenment, has postponed enlightenment in order to save as many others as he can. It is a sacrificial love which denies self to be enlightened so that one can continually work for the good of others.[17]

Confucianism entered Korea at about the same time as Buddhism. The fundamental principle of Confucianism teaches humans to be aware of their relations with others. There are five relationships: between father and son, ruler and subjects, husband and wife, elder and younger, and between friends.[18] The Confucian virtues used to deal with others in these five relationships are affection, justice, reverence for others, fidelity, harmony and proper order in family and society. A person's dignity, according to the Confucian approach, is defined and measured by the quality of one's relationship with other human beings. Confucianism thus embraces a moral and ethical system, a code of conduct, a philosophy of life and interpersonal relationships, and a method of government.[19]

Animism has been a part of Korean life since prehistoric times. It is associated with nature worship and the mythical story which tells how the son of the supreme deity descended to earth, married a woman and founded the first Korean state. Today, Animistic practices can be seen in ceremonies conducted by a "mudang" or shaman, who wards off the evil spirit, sickness, and bad luck and who invokes good fortunes, prosperity, peace and happiness from the ancestral spirits.[20]

The Catholic Church in Korea is marked by its unique origin, a series of horrifying persecutions and its amazingly rapid growth. Unlike other countries, Catholicism in Korea was initiated not by the missionary efforts of foreigners, but by a genuinely indigenous effort to embrace this non-Korean religious belief. The Koreans themselves planted the Catholic faith in Korea. It should be noted that from 1784 (when Fr. Matteo Ricci's "True Doctrine of God" was first brought into Korea) to 1794, (the year when Fr. Ju, Mun Mo-Jacques Vellozo came to Korea), the Korean Catholics had not had the help of any priest. During that decade, Korean Catholics grew to four thousand in number. When Fr. Jacques Vellozo was persecuted in 1810, the Korean Catholics, once again, had to practice their faith without the pastoral care of a priest, yet the number of Catholics steadily grew.

The documents concerning the early history of the Korean Catholic Church show that its members, despite the danger of official government persecution, in 1811 and in 1825 asked the Vatican to send missionaries. Such instances, in which indigenous faithful asked the Holy Father to send a priest, were unprecedented in Catholic church history.

The history of the Catholic Church in Korea would be incomplete without mentioning the contributions of the first Korean convert, Lee Seung Hun.[21] By the early 16th century, the Catholic Church had been firmly established in China, and writings on Catholicism were being widely read. In 1788, Lee went to China as a member of an official Korean envoy, and met Fr. Gramont in Beijing. There he was baptized. He returned to Korea with Catholic writings and religious artifacts. Most notably, he brought the "True Doctrine of God," which immediately attracted the attention of a small number of enlightened Korean scholar-gentry, who formed study groups. After returning from China, Lee baptized a handful of his associates, among them a widely respected scholar named Jung Yak Yong. These first Korean Catholics began religious services, without the presence of priests, at the home of Kim Bum Woo, in the capital's Myong-dong district.[22] Myong-dong remains, to this day, the symbol of the Korean Catholic Church. In 1785, this group of Korean Catholics became known to the government authorities, and Kim, as owner of the house of gathering, was jailed. Because of physical torture, he died several days after the arrest, becoming the first Korean Catholic martyr.

Lee Seung Hun and his fellow Catholics were so zealous and eager to spread their religious beliefs, without realizing the rules of Catholicism, that they literally "elected" a priest and a bishop among themselves. This first and last "election" in the history of the Catholic Church is not a laughing matter, but evidence of the early Korean Catholics' devotion.

Immediately after its creation, the Catholic Church of Korea faced opposition from the governing authorities. To the eyes of the government at this period, this strange new religion was downright heresy, contradictory to the ancestral traditions, and a possible pathway to dangerous foreign encroachment.[23] Accordingly, strong repressive measures were taken to uproot Christianity through a series of persecutions. Notable among these were the Four Great Persecutions (in 1801, 1839, 1846, and 1866). Each was marked by unparalleled brutality and atrocities. In 1801, the "Founding Fathers" of the Church, including Lee Seung Hun, were decapitated in public. Throughout this period every Christian was exposed to the constant threat of torture and death, but the faith miraculously survived.

After the last government decree in 1866, due to the unbending religious conviction and the missionary determination of the Korean Catholics, the persecution gradually subsided. Because of the many persecutions which they have endured, Korean Catholics take pride in the history of their Church. In 1984, Pope John Paul II went to Korea to canonize 103 early pioneers who shed their blood for Christ.

If we ask any Korean what he or she is like, one would not be surprised to find quite similar answers. The Korean people would tell us about the importance of family and social relationships, of education, and the approach to male and female roles and relationships. Korea, like many other Asian countries, is a hierarchically structured society. This is recognized in the forms of family and social interaction. As seen from relationships with others, behaviors of self-centeredness or selfishness are evil and cause disorder. The Korean has to relate with others in ways that rise above personal selfishness. Also in a relationship, the elder must receive prime respect from the younger; elders are treated with dignity and great respect. In a meeting situation, the younger ones must wait their turn to speak rather than openly and aggressively challenging the views of the elders. Since the society is so hierarchical, interaction is often formal. Traditional Confucian explanation for the formality is that there is a direct link between a person's inner disposition and his or her external disposition and conduct.[24]

Of the five key relationships, three deal with family. As it is for most of their Asian counterparts, the family is the center of everything for Koreans. A family is viewed as the single life force which is passed on from one generation to the next. This includes not only the living members but also the ancestors who have passed away. Children, then, are essentially the continuation or extension of the parents. In the family relation, the roles of man and woman, husband and wife, complement each other.[25] Also, in practice a woman enjoys complete autonomy in her own sphere of activity. She runs the household and controls the finances. A successful marriage is seen when a woman completes her responsibility in accommodating well in her new family. She does not disrupt the harmony and serves her in-laws dutifully. Success is also seen when a son is born into a family. A deep affectionate relationship often develops between a husband and wife; but the more essential ingredient is complete responsibility to the relationship, which is expected from both husband and wife.[26]

A Korean also views education as one of the highest values.[27] However, education according to the traditional Confucian approach is not only focused on excellence in academics, but also toward education for moral excellence. If a person lacks moral principles in relationships, academic excellence is useless.

Immigration to the United States

It is difficult to tell when the first group of Koreans entered the United States. However, during 1903 to 1920, it is reported that some 8,000 Koreans came into this country, mostly to the territory of Hawaii. In his book, *Strangers from A Different Shore —A History of Asian Americans*, Ronald Takaki describes the Korean immigrants: "Like the Chinese and Japanese, the Korean migrants were young: over 90 percent of the adults were between the ages of sixteen and forty-four. But unlike the first two groups of Asian immigrants, Koreans came from diverse walks of life. They were farmers, common laborers in the cities, government clerks, students, policemen, miners, domestic servants, and even Buddhist monks. Most of them were from urban areas rather than the country. In their level of education, they were more like the Japanese than the Chinese. About 70 percent of them were literate."[28]

Several things motivated Koreans to leave their homeland. The major reasons were the political and economic upheavals at home, including Japan's invasion and

1910 annexation.[29] This motivated many Koreans to leave their country to find freedom in the United States. Many who had joined the Independence Movement in Korea also had to flee for their lives. They became political refugees and sailed off to this new land.

As it had done to other Asians, poverty also drove Koreans to the United States.[30] Korea had been through a period of famine; the people were poor. Even the demands of hard work in the Hawaiian sugar cane plantations provided better opportunities than at home. The Koreans learned from advertisements and posters that a plantation worker in Hawaii would receive free housing, medical care, and sixteen dollars a month—a small fortune to them. Such economic opportunity was attractive and better than living in poverty.

Many Koreans who had converted to Christianity were encouraged by missionaries to emigrate to the United States. About 40 percent of Koreans who were Christians entered the United States during the early period of migration to this country.[31] The reasons for encouragement to emigrate were perhaps modern education, and humanistic and democratic ideals of liberal education. Another group of people who arrived in the early period were the Korean women who came as picture brides: women who were arranged for marriage through photographs sent to Korean men in Hawaii.[32] For many of these women, Hawaii gave them a promise of a better life and a better future.

After their arrival in the United States, the Korean people discovered that the demands of hard work were greater than they had expected. Many found hardships and disappointment on Hawaii's plantations, and decided to leave for the mainland. There, they were dispersed to work in the copper mines in Utah, coal mines in Colorado and Wyoming, railroads in Arizona, and even the salmon fisheries in Alaska. Many, however, settled in California.[33] If they lived in the cities, employment opportunities were restricted to services like janitorial, restaurant services, and domestic works. The job opportunities outside the cities were either employment with the railroad or work on the farms. The majority of Koreans were farm workers. Life on the farm, as extremely hard as it could be, was still another chance for a new life. Like other Asian immigrants in the early period of migration, the Koreans found themselves victims of discrimination by the state. They were restricted by the Asiatic Exclusion League

> "*I* want my children to grow up in the public school environment, not in the secluded private schools like Catholic school. But to be frank with you I am recently debating with myself on this point because I hear many incidents of violence, crime and drugs at the public schools. I can't imagine students beating their teachers. But sad enough that is the fact. Therefore, if I am financially comfortable and can find a good Catholic school in my neighborhood, most probably I'll send my children to Catholic school."
>
> **A Korean parent**

44

which condemned Korean and Japanese as undesirable aliens. President Theodore Roosevelt, in a 1907 executive order, prohibited the migration of Japanese and Korean laborers to the mainland from Hawaii. The Democratic Party in California called for "immediate federal legislation for the exclusion of Japanese, Korean and Hindu laborers" in 1912. The Alien Land Act of 1913 prohibited Koreans from owning or leasing land in California.[34]

One important factor which bound the Koreans together in this early period of migration was their struggle against the Japanese colonialism in their homeland. They felt as if they were the people with no country. The shared experience of the struggle for freedom of their own people at home gave them a sense of nationalistic unity and pride. This was a common bond that helped to establish independence movements and organizations in the United States as well.[35]

However, as time passed on into the second generation, many of the young Korean Americans began to drift away from their parents' determined nationalism. Their lives were surrounded by activities of typical American children.[36] They discovered not only the widening of the generation gap, but of the cultural gap as well.

The United States today still attracts Koreans seeking better opportunities. Like the early Koreans before them, many professional Korean people continue to arrive and make this land their home.

A Korean American Catholic Community

Like other Asian counterparts after the 1965 changes in United States immigration legislation, the Koreans were also immigrating into this country to seek better opportunities. Since 1980, close to half of all legal immigrants to the United States have come from Asia. A substantial number of Korean immigrants has settled in major metropolitan areas like Los Angeles, San Francisco, New York and Chicago. Unlike other Asian immigrants, however, Koreans are dispersed throughout the United States and Canada.[37] Many Catholic Koreans are among the new immigrants who come to the United States.

Approximately sixty Korean Catholic communities or "centers" have been established in the United States. A Korean Catholic community refers to the Catholic population of an area. Each community can be centered around a diocese, a center or a mission, a Korean community within a parish, or a Korean personal parish. These communities are led by Korean priests, Korean permanent deacons or lay leaders. The bishops in Korea have provided more than fifty Korean priests to minister to the Korean Catholic communities throughout the United States.[38] In June 1989, the United States Catholic Conference formally approved the "Standardized Agreement for Use with Bishops' Conferences of Other Countries for the Exchange of Clergy" with the Korean Episcopal Conference. In practice, this agreement has already been carried out for a few years.

The Korean priests have found their ministry to Korean Catholics in this country very challenging, according to Father Augustine Park, the Director of the National

Pastoral Center for the Korean Apostolate in the United States, and the Delegate of the Korean Episcopal Conference's Migration Pastoral Committee. In his "Report on the Pastoral Care of Korean Immigrants," he remarked that many Korean priests are involved not only with sacramental ministry, the regular Sunday Mass, and the catechumenate program, but also with various groups that practice devotional activities. Traditional practices like Legion of Mary, Cursillo, charismatic prayer groups, and marriage encounters also demand much of their time. The reason for such strong participation by the Korean people is that they see the church as the focal point of their lives in this new home. Korean Catholics often take pride in the "success" of their church communities and are willing to devote time and energy to parish activities. Korean priests and religious who are involved in the Korean ministry in this country often find themselves overwhelmed. Often they have too much responsibility for one person to carry.[39]

> "*In order to be a Catholic, you have to be a Korean first.*"
> **A Korean parish minister**

Korean American Catholic communities face many issues and concerns. Father Anthony Mortell in his paper "Korean Catholic Community in the United States" has noted a few important issues.[40] One concerns the local bishop. What is the attitude of the local bishop who one day encounters a growing non-Anglo Catholic community in his diocese? What kind of a structure should he give to this group of Catholics who come under his care? Would it be a Korean personal parish? Would it be a Korean Catholic center or mission? Would it be attached to some local parish, sharing the facility with other parishioners, a community within the larger faithful community? Or would he set out a policy in which the Korean Catholics have to integrate into the community at large, no matter what? Many important aspects, including finances, personnel, and political concerns, have to be considered in answering such questions. According to Rev. Augustine Park, who has 18 years of administrative and pastoral experience in the Korean Catholic Community, the ability to build personal parishes is the most important issue facing Korean communities today.

This leads to Father Mortell's second point: the location and organization of the various communities.[41] Everything in the Catholic Church always happens in the local parish. Conflicts such as accommodating schedules for two ethnic groups (or more) that share the same facility, language and cultural barriers, personnel (lack of an Asian priest), differences of ecclesiology as expressed in liturgies, pious devotions, and in attitude of welcoming, are issues that often contribute to tensions in the local parish.

Others issues that affect the Korean American Catholic communities are acculturation issues. As in other Asian communities, the children of the second generation feel that they are more American than Korean. Besides the widening of the generation gap, both parents and children experience a widening of a cultural gap. There is more and more a need for counselling services related to cultural values. The children often do not see the Eastern and Western world views as being compatible. It is often reported that the Church is the focal point for many of the first generation Koreans to gather for social and cultural unity. Since many feel lost in the alien American culture, they seek the church for cultural socialization—not strictly for religious reasons, but also to relieve loneliness and isolation. What will this do to the Korean American Catholic community in the long run? To put it in a positive term, how does evangelization fit into the process?

Evangelization will continue to be an issue facing the Korean American Catholic communities as long as the church still attracts other Koreans. The Korean lay people have always taken pride in their responsibility for the church. They will continue to play an important role in various ministries in their own local churches.

How long will the Korean bishops continue to send their priests and sisters into this country? The lack of vocations to the priesthood and religious life from the Korean American Catholic communities is another big concern.

Father Augustine Park stresses the urgency of cooperation on all levels of the people in the Church. He concludes in his report: "The seeds of the faith were first sewn in Korea two hundred years ago. The faith grew strong, having been nurtured by the blood of many Korean martyrs. Subsequently, missionaries were sent to Korea from America and other lands to minister to the Korean faithful, which has grown to nearly two million Catholics today. While vocations to the priesthood and religious life in Korea are not abundantly plentiful, God has blessed Korea with a diligent and dedicated native clergy. Korea must recognize its responsibilities to its people who have left the country to settle in other lands, and particularly, the hundreds of thousands who have emigrated to the United States and Canada. The Church in North America must join hands with the Church in Korea to develop pastoral care programs appropriate to the needs of the Korean ethnic community. The pastoral care of Korean immigrants in North America requires an urgent commitment and careful planning on the part of the U.S., Canadian, and Korean hierarchies. This special ministry urgently needs priests and religious who are well trained and suited to working with an immigrant community."[42]

Footnotes

1. H. Edward Kim. *Facts about Korea*, Holly Corporation, Seoul, Korea, 1985, pp. 24-25.
2. Ibid., pp. 34-36.
3. Ibid., p. 41.
4. Ibid., p. 46.
5. Ibid., p. 47.
6. Ibid., p. 51.
7. Ibid., p. 52.
8. Ibid., p. 54.
9. Ibid., p. 58.
10. Ibid., p. 66.
11. Ibid., p. 67.
12. Ibid., p. 74.
13. Ibid., p. 75.
14. Ibid., p. 75.

15. Ibid., p. 80.

16. R. Pierce Beaver, et al., ed., *Erdman's Handbook to the World's Religions*, Lion Publishing, England, 1983, p. 231.

17. Ibid., pp. 236-239.

18. To Thi Anh, *Eastern and Western Values, Conflict or Harmony?* East Asian Pastoral Institute, Manila, 1975, p. 16.

19. Michael C. Kalton, "Korean Ideas and Values," *Inculturation*, (Winter 1987), pp. 3-4.

20. *Facts about Korea*, p. 236.

21. Fr. Joseph Chang-mun Kim and Catechist John Jae-sun Chung, *Catholic Korea, Yesterday and Today*, Catholic Korea Publishing Co., Korea, 1964, p. 22.

22. Ibid., p. 27.

23. Ibid., pp. 31.

24. Kalton, "Korean Ideas and Values," pp. 5-7.

25. Ibid., p. 14.

26. Ibid., pp. 15-16.

27. Ibid., pp. 12-13.

28. Ronald Takaki, *Strangers from a Different Shore, A History of Asian Americans*, Little Brown and Company, Boston, 1989, p. 53.

29. Ibid., p. 54.

30. Ibid., p. 55.

31. Ibid., p. 53.

32. Ibid., p. 56.

33. Ibid., p. 270.

34. Ibid., p. 272.

35. Ibid., pp. 278-285.

36. Ibid., p. 286.

37. Robert W. Gardner, et al., *Asian Americans: Growth, Change, and Diversity*, Population Reference Bureau, Inc., Washington, DC, 1985, pp. 10-12.

38. Rev. Augustine Park, "A Report on the Pastoral Care of Korean Immigrants," 1985, p. 3.

39. Ibid., p. 6.

40. Rev. Anthony Mortell, SSC., "Korean Catholic Community in the United States, Present Status & Future Prospects," prepared for the third Annual Conference of Korean American University Professors Association, Los Angeles, November 1989, p. 13.

41. Ibid.

42. Park, "A Report on the Pastoral Care of Korean Immigrants," p. 6.

THE PHILIPPINES

Centuries before Spaniards discovered the Philippines, civilization already existed on the islands located in the Pacific Ocean, south of Taiwan and north of the Indonesian archipelago which included Borneo. In the third century B.C., these tropical islands were peopled by Malays who had immigrated from Indonesia and Malaya, and who were of northern Indian and Mongol origin. This immigration continued over the centuries, accompanied by smaller immigrations from China. Muslims also came, settling mostly in the southern islands. Intermarriages among these various groups gave birth to a native people who, centuries later, would be called Filipinos.

In 1469, Spanish monarchs began to finance expansion expeditions to unexplored parts of the world. Explorers were to bring home gold, spices and treasures from conquered lands and to spread Christianity.

Among the sixteenth century explorers Spain sent forth was Ferdinand Magellan, a Portuguese navigator who had transferred his allegiance to the Spanish crown. On September 20, 1519, he embarked on a voyage to the Spice Islands, taking a route that would go around the world. Rough seas forced Magellan to change his route, and after months at sea, Magellan and his men found themselves on the unnavigated seas of the Pacific. They continued despite many obstacles, passed Guam, and anchored on an unidentified island. Though this was not part of the Spice Islands, Magellan and his men saw enough gold and spices to make them decide to stay and conquer the islands, which were as yet not formed into a nation. It was easy to conquer these frightened natives, but the natives on neighboring islands led by Lapu-lapu, fought back. Magellan died during that battle.

Another expedition soon followed. By 1565, the Spaniards had succeeded in their two-fold goal of conquest and evangelization. They named the islands the Philippines after King Philip II. In later centuries, Dutch and other European explorers invaded the Philippines, with no success. With the help of Filipinos, the Spanish era continued uninterrupted for approximately four centuries.

The Spanish colonizers brought missionaries. With the union of church and state, churchmen were also government officials. The spiritual and temporal ruler was the Spanish king, who ruled from Spain. He appointed government and church leaders, assigned missionaries their own specific territories, established parishes and dioceses, and financed the development of both the church and the country.

The long Spanish rule deeply affected Filipino history, culture, character and faith-life. Though there were many abuses and injustices, the Spaniards contributed much that was good. They not only brought Christianity, but they also educated, taught more productive farming methods, and established law and order. Natives were encouraged to resettle in new villages built around the church, which became the center of the people's religious, social, educational and cultural activities. Thus, civilization advanced more rapidly.

The strong union of church and state throughout the Spanish rule led to excessive abuses and neglect of the proper development of the Filipinos as a people with equal rights as human beings. Native vocations were discouraged because Filipinos were considered inferior, not worthy to join the ranks of the Spanish friars. Suppression of basic human rights slowly fired the spirit of nationalism and moved the Filipinos to assert their rights and take their rightful place in the church. This movement toward nationalism caused a group of native clergy to separate from the Church. A new religion was formed and schism was declared.

Revolution finally ended the Spanish era. In 1898, the American fleet came to the rescue of the Philippines. On December 10, 1898, the Treaty of Paris ceded the Philippines to the United States. This marked the end of one historical era and the beginning of another.

With Spanish bishops and friars banished from the Philippines, the Filipino church reached its lowest point. The absence of leadership, the schism, and the well-financed efforts of American Protestant missionaries confused the people. To revitalize the Filipino church, the Apostolic See sent American bishops to lead. American missionaries were sent, to continue the work of evangelization and to counteract the Protestant missionaries' successful proselytizing methods. Newly arrived priests and sisters built schools and taught English; education became very competitive and reached a high level.

> *"I see Filipino youth and young adults who feel that the Church is an old fashioned, unbending, unforgiving entity that does not respond to their need to be included, or to be among friends. They see a Catholic Church that does not teach that 'Each day is a walk with the Lord.'"*
>
> **A Filipino youth minister**

When the American military rule ended in 1901, Americans slowly introduced a democratic government. In 1934, the Tydings-McDuffie Act was signed, providing for a ten-year transitional period, at the end of which the Philippines would be granted independence. This transition period was broken by the Japanese invasion in 1941. Fighting beside American troops, Filipinos helped the Allies win World War II. Independence was finally granted in 1946. But the Philippines continued to depend on the United States for political and economic help. The leaders of the newly independent country needed continued guidance in making democracy work, and the country was ravaged by the war. Thus, the close ties between the United States and the Philippines continued.

Democracy in the Philippines was threatened early on, by the insurgence of a Communist Party known as Hukbalahab, or Huks. This threat was contained and democracy continued until September, 1972, when President Ferdinand Marcos declared martial law. The Philippines thus became a dictatorship ruled by Marcos until late 1985. President Marcos, confident of his absolute power and hold on the

Filipino people, announced that he would call for a presidential election in early 1986. The Filipino people nominated a housewife inexperienced in politics but whose popularity grew after the assassination of her husband, a political enemy of Marcos. The official count of the election watchdog, NAMFREL, declared Mrs. Corazon Aquino the winner while the opposition insisted Marcos had won.

A revolution ensued. But the potentially bloody election became a peaceful revolution. The Filipino people, holding statues of Mary above their heads, took to the streets and confronted the heavily armed military with prayers, songs of praise to Mary and Jesus, kindness and compassion for the soldiers ordered to kill them, flowers and food. It was a celebration of faith and goodness. The people power, rooted in the people's faith in God and in their quest for peace and justice, toppled the well-financed and well-armed Marcos regime.

The euphoria of the peaceful revolution is long past, and the country is left with the social maladies that have plagued the Philippines for centuries. The majority of the people are under poverty level; unemployment and underemployment are on the rise; the gap between rich and poor becomes even wider with the diminishing middle class; the infant mortality rate has increased because of malnutrition; and crime continues to disturb peace and order. Political instability undermines economic development. How long can democracy last under such economic, social and political strain?

The answer is that the faith, the hope, and the courage of the Filipino people will pull them through this most critical time, just as in the past.

The Filipino People

Religion

Pre-hispanic Filipinos, predominantly of Malay and Muslim origin, were familiar with metal tools and were skilled in pottery making, basket weaving, and carving. They lived simply as fishermen, farmers, and hunters. They were animists, regarding natural calamities as displeasure of their gods or their ancestral spirits, called *anitos*. Their natural affinity to nature was reflected in their belief in a mighty creator, *Bathalang Maykapal*. He was a distant god and natives believed that the way to reach him was through their *anitos*. As an expression of gratitude, commitment and loyalty to their *anitos*, natives worshipped them through rituals, nature feasts, charms and other symbols.

The Spanish missionaries who accompanied Magellan were largely concerned with Christianizing the natives, by force if necessary. Evangelization began in earnest with the second expedition which brought more missionaries, who were assigned to all parts of the archipelago. In attracting the natives to the faith, the missionaries built on the natives' love for the spectacular, through plays and dramatic homilies. Elaborate *fiestas* and processions were held on special occasions, particularly during the feastday of the town's patron saint. During Holy Week, the passion was reenacted to emphasize Christ's sufferings. Because the Christian symbols had parallels in the pagan rituals and celebrations, Christianity became

51

more acceptable to the natives.

Although outwardly accepting the Catholic faith, the natives never really understood it. At times they celebrated their pagan rituals clandestinely out of fear, and other times they incorporated old rituals into the new religion. This gave rise to a popular religion, called folk Catholicism, which grew rapidly because there were so few missionaries to pursue evangelization and religious formation.

Ironically, this popular religiosity kept the Filipino people's faith alive between 1899 and 1903, when the church was without leadership. This was the time of the great revolution marking the end of the Spanish era and the schism that divided the native clergy. Practically every diocese was without any bishop; Spanish friars were either in prison or unable to leave Manila, while the Filipino people went to the mountains to join the guerillas. Seminaries were closed and the people practiced folk Catholicism freely.

The situation has not changed much today. *The National Directory of the Philippines* prepared by the Episcopal Commission on Education and Religious Formation offers this profile of Filipino Catholics:

> The majority of Filipinos are not adequately catechized. Broad segments of our population lack adequate systematic instruction in the faith.... The majority has been initiated into Christian life by the reception of the sacraments of baptism and confirmation. Most still desire to have their marriages blessed in the sacrament of matrimony, and to receive the last anointing of the sick—although culturally this is still held off until the last moment. Hence, the average Filipino Catholic can be said to be sacramentalized—baptized, confirmed and married in the Church. But preparation for these sacraments, and for the Christian life in general, still leaves much to be desired.... This brief sketch indicates that a very great number of both rural and urban Filipino Catholics are at the level of catechumens, i.e., in need of systematic catechesis toward maturing in the faith.

Culture

Unlike many of its neighbors, the Philippines has no ancient culture to claim as its own. The Filipino culture is a mixture of many eastern and western cultures. It is still in the process of becoming. A poet compared Filipino culture to the *tinikling*. In *tinikling*, dancers dance between clashing bamboo poles, taking care that their feet are not caught. The Filipino culture is a dance between two cultures—the east and the west—and Filipinos take care not to be caught by the clashing elements of the two cultures.

The Filipino sees time as cyclical and dynamic, moving slowly, the past becoming part of the present and the future. In contrast, westerners view time as moving rapidly, in linear progress of past, present and future.

Filipino philosophy of law differs from the way Americans regard law. While Americans tend to stress their rights in relation to law, Filipinos emphasize duties in their hierarchical society, starting with the family. This has to do with the authoritarian nature of Philippine society in which people see themselves more as subjects with duties to fulfill than as individuals with basic rights.

Writing and signing contracts is not a regular practice of Filipinos, who learned the value of the word of honor from early Chinese traders. Because Filipinos do not emphasize written laws or contracts, law is often viewed interiorly, and responsibility to uphold the law comes from within. Thus the implementation of the law is connected with the value of *utang na loob* or debt of gratitude or volition, often lasting a lifetime. Filipinos tend to regard law subjectively rather than absolutely. Exceptions to the law are often made, usually in favor of the rich and those in authority and power.

Religion is so integrated into Filipino life that it is often difficult to distinguish the social from the religious in big celebrations. Are privileged moments of life—baptism, confirmation, weddings, funerals—social events or religious celebrations? It is sometimes difficult to distinguish, especially when the reception after the event receives more time and attention than the actual religious event.

Filipino culture is further characterized by the culture of shame or *hiya*, as a direct result of long years of western colonization. Following a long history of subjugation, *hiya* has become a major sanction or motivating factor in Filipino behavior. It is based primarily on social or peer pressure; often, decisions are made because of *hiya* and not because of personal conviction. What others will say often becomes more important than what is the right thing to do.

Filipinos are not confrontive by nature and they value smooth interpersonal relationships. They like to preserve harmony whenever possible; go-betweens or intermediaries are often used when there is a possible confrontation or sensitive issue to discuss. Euphemistic language is employed to help prevent arguments. To preserve smooth interpersonal relationships, together with *hiya*, Filipinos tend to say "yes" or "maybe" even when they mean "no."

Hospitality is a mark of the Filipino culture. Filipinos go out of their way to extend hospitality to visitors and friends, who can drop in any time without prior notice and take part in the family meal. The Filipino's spontaneous smile and friendliness bring warmth and welcome even to strangers.

Values

The family as a harmonious unit is a primary Filipino value. The Episcopal Commission on Education and Religious Instruction of the Bishops' Conference of the Philippines explains this in the *National Catechetical Directory*:

The Filipino family plays a pivotal role in the life of the individual and society—its influence is pervasive. Despite rapid changes taking place and the influence of modernization, the family remains the most stable unit of society. For Filipinos, their families are their most important reference group, the core of their alliance system where they find strength, security and support. Loyalty to family and kin, family solidarity and togetherness in addition to concern for family welfare and honor, rank high in priorities.

The Filipino family is still predominantly rural, agricultural and traditional...a closely knit, protective and personalistic unit. Strong ties of loyalty bind Filipinos to their in-groups, and their familial *utang na loob* lasts throughout life.... Their interdependence among familial relationships is a major characteristic of the Filipino family.

Within the Filipino family there is a hierarchy of authority. Formal authority resides in the father, but decision making is shared by the mother, who holds the purse strings. The eldest in the family, whether boy or girl, has the greatest responsibility for caring for the younger ones. Respect for elders remains a high value; family solidarity is stressed—brothers and sisters are close to one another and interdependence among them is encouraged.

> *"We came to the U.S. Because of better economic opportunity, better education, better future for our children. We want to be integrated in the local church and at the same time we want to recognize our cultural heritage."*
> **Filipino parents**

Filipino families, noted for their child-centeredness, tend to be large, especially in rural areas. Since most Filipino children grow up with many others in the house, including adults besides their parents, they are seldom left alone. Hence, quite early Filipino children learn to look to others for their needs, to submit to the will of others, to be grateful, and to control their feelings of hostility. Most Filipino children grow up to be sensitive, tactful, but relatively unassertive.

Filipino parents in general are indulgent and affectionate toward their children. When the child is of school age, parents become more demanding. Obedience is expected and the adage, 'children are seen, but not heard,' is still held by the majority of Filipino parents, though with modernization the youth begin to question and assert themselves.

In the Filipino family, elders are respected as persons of authority and wisdom, as individuals who deserve special love and care because of the love and care they have given their children and grandchildren. Elderly parents are cared for by their children and are rarely sent to convalescent homes.

Filipino family extends beyond the nuclear unit to include relatives, neighbors, and friends. Because these strong extended families and friendships offer support and assistance in times of need, a welfare system such as that in the United States is unnecessary, and homelessness is rare.

Education is another primary Filipino value. Parents make great sacrifices to send their children to the best schools. When financial resources are limited, parents will send at least one child to college, with the other children helping to make this possible. The ultimate goal is to migrate to a foreign country, particularly the United States, where job opportunities are better. With a good and steady income, immigrants send money home to support parents and to educate brothers and sisters.

Underlying all these values is the Filipinos' deep and personal faith which sustains them through difficult times, strengthens them in critical moments, and gives them hope even when things and events seem impossible. This faith is expressed in the family altar that is displayed prominently in homes of rich and poor alike. It is the same faith that has accompanied the Filipinos throughout their history of development as a people and as a nation.

Immigration to the United States

F ilipinos first immigrated to the United States in the early part of the twentieth century when young men, mostly from the northern part of the Philippines, were recruited as cheap labor for plantations in Hawaii, agricultural fields of California, and mess halls of the United States Navy. They were considered as U.S. nationals because the Philippines was then a U.S. colony. As nationals, they received the rights of citizens except the right to vote, own property, and marry as they chose. But even when they finally received these rights, Filipino nationals were still underpaid and forced to live in poor residential areas in non-white American districts. Discrimination was very strong.

American colonization naturally brought about intermarriages between American military men and Filipino women. When Filipino nationals had the opportunity to go home, they did so, and married. Eventually, members of the increasingly Filipino-American families in the Philippines were allowed to enter the United States legally as immediate families of American citizens.

In the 1950s, the Exchange Visitors' Program for medical graduates opened the doors to Filipino professionals. Young Filipino doctors received medical internships in hospitals—notably in New York, Illinois, Michigan, California and Washington—and were helped to obtain permanent residency afterwards. The lack of nurses in American hospitals motivated young Filipino high school graduates to enroll in nursing and other medical-related fields. With a bachelor's degree in such fields, a Filipino professional had a relatively easy time applying for a permanent visa to the United States. Those in other professions were also able to seek legal entry. This exodus started what has been called a brain drain from the Philippines.

After the passage of the 1965 Immigration Act—which provided, among other things, higher visa quotas for the Philippines and family reunification—Filipino immigration to the United Stated increased rapidly. Early Filipino immigrants petitioned for members of their immediate families to join them in the United States. After becoming naturalized American citizens, these immigrants petitioned for their parents who, in turn, became citizens and petitioned for their unmarried children under age 21. This pattern of immigration, marriages and births has meant steady growth in the Filipino-American population. In the 1970s, and especially after Marcos declared martial law, more Filipino immigrants arrived, further increasing the Filipino population. This group included political refugees, businessmen, investors, traders, students and tourists. Most of them have remained permanently.

The Filipino-American population has grown so rapidly that in 1985 Filipinos had displaced Chinese, nationally, as the largest Asian-American group. With the continued increase in population, Filipinos will remain the largest Asian group in the United States, with a total population, by the year 2000, of 2,070,571. This represents 21% of this country's Asian community. Filipinos most often settle in California, Illinois, Michigan, New Jersey, Washington, Florida and Texas.

The Filipino Catholic Community

Like most immigrants, Filipinos come to the United States for different reasons, mainly economic and political. Approximately eighty-five percent of Filipino immigrants have been born into the Catholic faith. Most fit into the Philippine Bishops' Conference's general description mentioned earlier: most are sacramentalized but not catechized, bringing with them a traditional faith that revolves around devotions, sacramentals and rituals.

The Filipino Catholic immigrant comes to the United States with a unique experience of church. Parishes in the Philippines are much bigger than the average American parish, with an average population of 20,000 to 50,000, and one priest for every 10,000 Catholics. Rural parishes are composed of eleven or more islands, or one big town with several villages. In densely populated cities like Manila, some churches are clustered together with ill-defined boundaries. They are filled to capacity on Sundays, and personal interaction between priests and parishioners is often almost impossible. Thus, people are not generally concerned about parish affiliations. They attend Mass anywhere they want, with no specific responsibility toward that church.

Begun as a missionary church, the church in the Philippines depended on Spain for financial support throughout the Spanish era, giving the people the impression that the church was rich. Even after the Spanish regime, financial support continued to help European missionaries establish missions and apostolates. Not until the missionary status of the Philippine Church was removed were Filipino Catholics asked to assume some of the financial responsibilities. The main source of income came primarily from stole fees. Considering the volume of weddings, baptisms and funerals in a parish with 50,000 Catholics, the sacramental fees made up for the lack of regular Sunday contributions.

In this style of parish life and church support, there has been no need for registration and Sunday envelopes. It is outside the average Filipino's parish experience to register; and using Sunday envelopes is not part of the cultural system. When Filipino immigrants continue this pattern in the United States, it is often perceived as a lack of willingness to participate in parish life, even if the Filipinos faithfully fulfill their Sunday obligation. Some pastoral ministers regard it as indifference. Whatever it may be called, it is a sign that Filipino Catholics have not yet adjusted to the U.S. style of church life.

Another reason for Filipino immigrants' seeming passivity in parish life is the lack of inclusivity toward Filipinos in their parishes, particularly if the parish is not open to their particular faith expressions. According to the Episcopal Commission on Education and Religious Instruction, "Filipino Catholicism has always...[stressed]...rites and ceremonies. *Fiestas*, processions, pilgrimages, novenas, innumerable devotional practices...mark the concrete devotional practice of Filipino Catholics. Much of what they know of Christian doctrinal truths and moral values is learned through these sacramental and devotional practices."

The *Pastoral Plan for Filipino Ministry* of the Archdiocese of San Francisco writes about the Filipino lack of participation in parish life:

Because of long years of foreign rule and support, the Filipino tends to be dependent, looking for one who will do things for him, tell him what to do, give him approval, give him material, emotional and psychological support especially in times of crisis. [Thus]...the Filipino does not volunteer in the parish. He takes on a responsibility only when the pastor or pastoral minister personally asks him. He hesitates to make his needs known to the parish, but expects the parish to fill his needs, articulate them for him, and offer the right response.

The most convenient reason given for lack of participation of the Filipino in the parish is shyness or innate reticence. It is, however, deeper than that. It is the deeply ingrained paternalism and colonial mentality obscuring the Filipino's natural sense of community (*pagkamakatao*) and spirit of cooperation (*pakikisama*). The debilitating sense of insecurity and inferiority prevents him from graciously and naturally accepting a compliment, from recognizing his value to the parish community, and from interacting with the other parishioners with confidence and sense of well-being.

Throughout the historical process of the Filipino, the larger society, in general, has not treated him kindly as an individual. As a result, the Filipino has learned to look for security and appreciation from [his] small reference group. This is the main reason for the small-group orientation of the Filipino. In the parish, he seeks the company of...fellow Filipinos with whom he can be himself and with whom he feels equal. He is most free and alive when he is with a small group speaking the same native language, experiencing the same struggles as immigrants from a developing country, and celebrating significant events in their traditional faith. These groupings of Filipinos are to be used as natural ways of giving them a sense of belonging and confidence in the parish.

Without the familiar Philippine Catholic environment and without understanding the new American church and environment, they [Filipinos] feel lost in the church. They alienate themselves from the parish as they look for Filipino priests who can minister to them on a personal basis and for religious groups which are willing to accept them and their traditional faith.

The Church should look at this reality with great concern and compassion. The absence of traditional faith in an American parish...leaves a vacuum in the faith-life of Filipino immigrants, especially those whose only experience of faith is popular piety. The vacuum must be filled immediately. It must be filled using Filipino culture as a point of evangelization.

As Filipinos' pastoral needs are articulated, the church in the United States is slowly encouraging and initiating the development of the pastoral care of Filipinos. Four dioceses—San Francisco, Chicago, Oakland, and Honolulu—have established diocesan offices for the Filipino apostolate. Other dioceses and individual parishes are beginning to be aware of the importance of a responsive Filipino ministry to meet the pastoral Filipino Catholic immigrants' needs and to bring them into the mainstream of parish life. They also recognize the Filipino faith as important to the life and vitality of the Church.

The National Conference of Catholic Bishops of the United States (NCCB) officially recognized the beginning of a national pastoral ministry to Filipinos with the First National Convention of Filipino Apostolate on January 12 to 15, 1990. The convention was held in the Archdiocese of San Francisco through the initiative of the Office of Pastoral Care of Migrants and Refugees, Bishops' Committee on Migration of the NCCB/USCC. Eighteen dioceses participated in the three-day convention where the needs of the Filipino Catholic Community of the United States were articulated and plans for a National Pastoral Center, under the auspices of the NCCB/USCC, were discussed. A spirit of collaboration, joy, hope, and deep faith characterized the historic event. It was a new beginning, a big and warm gesture of the church's welcome to Filipino Catholics, an invitation to walk together in renewing the church and a sign of respect for the Filipino faith and culture.

CAMBODIA, LAOS, VIETNAM

Indochina (1893-1954)

Indochina refers to the Southeast Asian countries that came under French domination in the 19th century: Cambodia, Laos and Vietnam. Although the peoples of these countries come from perhaps the most linguistically and ethnically diverse regions in the world, the majority group in each country is ethnically homogeneous.[1] Today the term Indochina is rejected by the people from Cambodia, Laos and Vietnam because of its colonial connotations.[2]

These countries were opened to Western influences as early as the 16th century. Not until the 19th century did the French begin to colonize the Indochinese peninsula. In 1867, Cochin, China, a part of Vietnam today, came under the French colony. France established protectorates that dominated Cambodia in 1863. Annam and Tonkin, two states that are also part of present-day Vietnam, became part of the French colonization in 1884. These states were united and proclaimed as the French Indochinese Union in 1887, led by a French governor general. In 1893, Laos finally came under this alliance.[3]

During World War II, Indochina briefly became part of the Japanese Empire.[4] At that time, Vietnamese nationalism began to form, and the Indochina Communist party was established. It joined force with another anti-colonial nationalist movement, the Vietnam Independence League (Vietminh), to resist the Japanese. When Japan began to lose the war, the French announced a plan to revive the Union. Under this plan, each member state was allowed greater self-government. While Cambodia and Laos accepted this proposal, the Vietnamese nationalists called for complete independence from French domination to unite Cochin, China in the south, Annam in the center, and Tonkin in the north. This was the beginning of the French Indochina War in 1946. The war lasted almost a decade, ending with the massive French defeat at Dien Bien Phu in 1954. An international conference in Geneva mandated the withdrawal of all foreign troops from Cambodia and Laos. It called for a temporary partition of Vietnam on the 17th parallel, which created the Democratic Republic of Vietnam in the north and the Republic of Vietnam in the south. It also mandated reunification of Vietnam with a national representative government to be achieved by supervised general elections in 1956. The elections did not occur. The South Vietnamese President Ngo Dinh Diem, supported by an American government seeking an anti-Communist base in Southeast Asia, canceled the elections.[5]

The United States' Involvement

D uring the Second World War, with American logistical support, the Vietminh fought the Japanese until their surrender in 1945. In the face of French plans to revive the French Indochinese Union, U.S. policy favored Vietnamese nationalism.

For the United States government, mainland China's 1949 move to communism transformed the French Indochina War from colonial struggle to anti-communist struggle. For the next twenty-five years, the United States committed itself militarily and politically to maintaining Indochina's non-communist regimes.[6]

South Vietnam's President Ngo Dinh Diem canceled the elections that would have reunited the partitioned country. Soon thereafter, the National Liberation Front (Viet Cong) was established, with the support of Ho Chi Minh, to start the guerilla warfare against the Ngo Dinh Diem government. Their cause was reunification of North and South Vietnam. Through the administrations of Presidents Kennedy, Johnson and Nixon, the United States committed enormous amounts of manpower and resources to preserve the independence of South Vietnam's government.[7] In 1975, South Vietnam shifted to communist rule.

Shortly after this, Cambodia and Laos also moved into communist rule. These communist take-overs have caused hundreds of thousands of people from Vietnam, Laos and Cambodia to flee their countries. From 1975 to 1989, according to the Office of Refugee Resettlement, U.S. Department of Health and Human Services, 930,158 refugees from these three countries came to the United States.[8]

Cambodia, Laos, Vietnam: History

Cambodia

C ambodia's recorded history began in the 1st century A.D., when Hindu kingdoms ruled the land, calling it Funan.[9] After 400 years of Indian influenced rule, the native Khmer people took over and established the Angkor empire. The Angkor period, which began in the ninth century and extended to the 15th century, saw great accomplishments in arts, culture, architecture and literature. At its peak, the Angkor empire included much of present day Cambodia, Thailand, Laos and Vietnam. The temple known as Angkor Wat, built during this period, is one of the seven wonders of the world. The Wat symbolizes the beauty and greatness of Angkor's advanced culture.[10]

As the thirteenth century waned, the Angkor civilization disintegrated into smaller kingdoms, often ruled by the Thais. There were many struggles for territory among the Thais, Cambodians and Vietnamese throughout the years.[11]

Cambodia was part of the French Indochinese Union from 1863 to 1954.[12] The Geneva Conference called for the withdrawal of all foreign troops from Cambodia. In its early years of independence, Cambodia was led by Prince Norodom Sihanouk. In 1970, Sihanouk was overthrown by General Lon Nol.[13] The Vietnam War was escalating and Cambodia became a target of U.S. attacks against military bases which the U.S. identified as Viet Cong. This spurred the growth of Cambodian communists, the Khmer Rouge. In 1975, the Khmer Rouge, led by Pol Pot, seized control of the country, and thus began the most tragic chapter of Cambodia's history. Renaming the country Kampuchea, and completely closing it off to all outsiders, the Khmer Rouge moved most Khmer to the countryside, where families were separated and forced to work on communal farms. Huge numbers of people were tortured and killed, particularly those who were educated and those who had any affiliation with either the former Cambodian government or the United States. Some two to three million Khmer are believed to have died in Pol Pot's holocaust.[14]

In 1979, Pol Pot's bloody regime ended as Vietnamese troops invaded Cambodia and installed a government headed by Heng Samrin. Thousands of Cambodians fled to Thailand. The Khmer Rouge fled to the hills and for the next decade conducted border military campaigns not only against the Vietnamese, but against other Khmer resistance forces led by Lon Nol and Prince Sihanouk. In 1988, Vietnam announced that it would withdraw from Cambodia by September, 1989.

Laos

In the 7th century A.D., people from the Yunnan area of China moved south, eventually spreading to much of modern-day Laos and Thailand. Many of today's Lao are descended from these early settlers. The history of the early Lao was one of clan wars fought to determine domination.[15] By 1707, there were three major Lao kingdoms. Seventy years later, the King of Thailand colonized the three kingdoms, and for more than a century, the Lao launched unsuccessful attempts to free themselves from Thai domination.

When France took control of Indochina, it incorporated Laos into the French Indochinese Union in 1893. The French pressured Thailand's king to relinquish some of the Lao territory. A 1907 treaty divided Laos into two nations, one under the French and the other under the Thai. During the Second World War, Japan took over Laos for a short period of time. After the Japanese surrender in 1945, France regained control. Many Lao leaders fled to Thailand to establish an independence movement called the "Free Movement."[16] In 1949, when France finally granted Laos greater independence, many of these leaders returned to help form the new government. Meanwhile, others who did not return started another movement known as the "Pathet Lao."[17] The power struggles to control the government began and continued even after Laos gained complete independence from France in 1954. The Geneva Conference mandated that all foreign troops withdraw from Laos. The power struggles continued, even after complete independence, until a 1962 coali-

> "*One of the difficulties of being parents is trying to protect the kids and yet try to leave them some freedom. They will say, 'Do not force prayer on me.' As a refugee parent we are so busy trying to survive. I have to work hard at work all day and when I get home I have to take care of my family.*"
> **A Vietnamese parent**

tion government was formed. This government received aid from the United States until 1973. By 1975, the communists had taken control of Laos. Thus, the exodus of Laotian refugees began. Among those refugees were thousands of Hmong, hill peoples who had migrated from China in the early 19th century. The CIA had recruited many Hmong to fight Viet Cong and Lao communist forces and to rescue downed American pilots during the secret war the U.S. waged in Laos.[18] When the Lao government fell to communism, the Hmong were also forced to flee.

Even though Laos' total population is small, there are many ethnic groups in Laos. The two major groups are the lowland Lao, which is the largest single group, and the highland Lao. The largest highland group is the Hmong community; other ethnic groups are Iu Mien, Kmhmu, Lahu, Lao Lue, and Lao Tinh.[19] Most of these ethnic groups remain autonomous with their own languages and cultures.

Vietnam

The Vietnamese are believed to be the descendants of Southern China's Mongoloid peoples, who moved southward and throughout the Red River Delta.[20] The Chinese conquered the area, and formed present-day northern Vietnam under its empire in the second century B.C. After many revolts, the Vietnamese successfully ended direct Chinese domination in 938 A.D.,[21] and founded their first national dynasty. Many Chinese invasions throughout the years were repelled, including troops from the Ming dynasty between 1406 and 1427. The last Chinese invasion before the French domination was in 1789, and it also was repelled.

Meanwhile, the Vietnamese people had begun to move westward and southward along the coasts toward the Me Khong Delta. Along the way, they either took over by force or absorbed the other peoples and kingdoms. Vietnamese westward expansion was impeded by a few factors, particularly by the Annamite mountains, which run parallel to the coast and define the shape of present day Vietnam. Many of the hill tribe peoples, such as the Hmong, Yao, Tia 'Pou Thai' and others, never accepted the Vietnamese. Nevertheless, the Vietnamese expanded into these regions and fought for domination. The struggles for domination by Vietnam, Laos, Cambodia and Thailand were persistent during different times and various kingdoms.

Vietnamese sovereignty ended with the 19th century French colonization of Indochina.[22] Initially, France took over Saigon in 1858 ostensibly to protect the Catholic missions. However, the take-over was mainly to establish a naval base. In 1883, France invaded and took Hanoi. In 1885, France established control over Vietnam, which was then divided into three regions: Tonkin in the north, Annam in the central part, and Cochin, China in the south. The rise of Vietnamese nationalism began. It was the beginning of the anti-colonialism movement which succeeded in gaining its independence at Dien Bien Phu in 1954.

The Peoples, Cultures and Religions of Cambodia, Laos, and Vietnam

The following excerpts are taken from *Cambodia: The Land and Its People* distributed by the Lutheran Immigration and Refugee Service.[23]

Culture and Customs

Cambodians are formal people; they appreciate well-educated and polite persons. They respond warmly to friendly approaches, and usually associate soft speaking voices with a cultured upbringing.

Cambodians aren't accustomed to shaking hands as a greeting, except those who were exposed to Western influences. To greet others they join their hands together and raise them to their foreheads, bowing their heads at the same time.

Touching between members of the same sex is common. For instance, two boys or two girls very often walk hand-in-hand as a sign of friendship.

Touching a person's head is not done, because Cambodians believe the head, the seat of consciousness, is the most sacred part of a human being. They believe that if you touch the head of a person, he won't be as clever as he should be and could even get sick. But if you know a family well, then you might touch, for instance, the heads of the children, or have them sit on your lap. Cambodians don't cross or walk under hanging clothes, especially women's pants or skirts.

The head of the family is traditionally greeted first, then his wife, with greetings continuing from the eldest to the youngest.

Among Cambodians, the terms Older Brother, Younger Brother, Uncle, Aunt, Niece, Nephew, Grandfather, Grandmother and so forth are used much more than first names, even when applied to persons who aren't relatives.

Cambodians are usually very shy. If you invite them to eat, even if they are hungry or starving, they will initially refuse. This is simply a "probe refusal" so as not to seem over-eager. It may be necessary to extend your offer 2 or 3 times so that they will know your invitation is not just a "courteous invitation."

Because life in Cambodia is leisurely, Cambodians may seem very slow here. They are not used to endless rushing.

Cambodians may also be superstitious. For instance, they might not want to be in a photo of three persons together, three representing an unlucky number.

The most popular sports in Cambodia are soccer, boxing, basketball, volleyball, bicycle races and ping-pong.

In rural areas, men and women generally wear loosely-draped turban-like head gear as protection against the hot sun when they work in the rice fields. Women wear a skirt called "sampot" which is black, or made of

63

multi-colored silk for formal dress in the day-time, or of only one color of silk. It is not polite to have a hat on indoors or while talking to older persons.

Cross-legged sitting and turning the back to someone while talking also are not considered polite.

In Cambodian culture, given names are sometimes chosen by astrologers. These names are chosen especially for the individual, for their meanings—which is why a person is addressed by his/her personal name. In official situations, however, persons are called by their family names first, and then the given names.

The formal Cambodian calendar is a combination of the lunar and solar calendars. That is, the months are based upon the movement of the moon, but the yearly cycle of months is corrected to bring them into accord with the sun's movement. The lunar months are also the basic units for the Cambodian religious calendar.

Religion

Buddhism: In Cambodia, Theravada Buddhism is the dominant religion, adhered to by nearly 90 percent of the population. There are two groups of Cambodian monks. They are the Mohanikay (greater congregation) and the Thammayut (the orthodox wing). Both sects use the same doctrine, but make different interpretations of some aspects, chiefly regarding monastic life. Buddhist doctrine preaches nonviolence and the extinction of passion, and stresses charity and humility. The doctrinal formula can be restated as follows: A man is the fruit of what he has been. Each past malicious deed or intent carries a seed which germinates into misfortune in the present life. Present misfortune can be traced to some misdeed committed in a previous existence.

Spirit Worship and Traditional Belief: Most Cambodians believe in superstitions, and the supernatural traditions combine animism, sorcery, naturalism and magical rites. The spirits include the "Neak Ta" (or cult of tutelary spirits), primarily the guardian spirits, which also possess an instinct and a power for malevolence and vengeance; and the "Katha," sacred Buddha figurines carved from ivory, iron pyrites, a wild boar tusk, or teeth of a parent, which are believed to possess magical power. Fortune tellers are very popular. They are consulted for future mates, for advice before making important political, economic or other decisions.

The Ruup Areak (spirit medium): Villagers may call upon the Ruup Areak to perform ceremonies at various times throughout the year and to communicate with the spirit world. The Khruu is believed to have a number of talents, often including curing, finding lost objects, brewing love potions, and making protective amulets.

The following excerpts are taken from *Evangelization in Cambodia*, by Rev. Rogatien Rondineau, MEP.[24]

The Gospel was first proclaimed in Cambodia in 1555. The early evangelization effort had limited success. By the middle of the 19th century, Catholics in Cambodia numbered about 500—half were Vietnamese and the other half were Cambodians and Chinese.

In the latter part of the 19th century, many Vietnamese fleeing the persecutions in their country entered Cambodia. In fewer than 80 years, a population of 250 Catholics grew to 60,000, scattered across the country. Many missionaries were unable to evangelize the Cambodians because they were too busy ministering to the Vietnamese. Besides, the simple but very efficient organization of the Buddhist villages, with people clustered around the pagoda where Buddhist monks lived, prevented the Cambodians from leaving their traditional way of life—Buddhism of "the Lesser Vehicle." By leaving their religious traditions, they would have excluded themselves from the mainstream of the village life.

In 1970, most of the Vietnamese returned to Vietnam with their priests, missionaries and most of the nuns. Only a handful of missionaries, the Cambodian priests, the Carmelites, the Benedictines and some sisters remained in Cambodia. During the war of 1969-1975, six missionaries were killed. Five communities of Cambodian Catholics received the assistance of priests. After Pol Pot's 1975 take-over, they all were scattered. The missionaries were expelled, the Cambodian priests were killed or died of starvation, and the religious Brothers and Sisters who remained in Cambodia were also killed. The Carmelites went into exile in Belgium. The churches were torn down. Absolutely no religious activity was possible.

Now, as far as we know, perhaps 1,500 Cambodian Catholics have survived in Cambodia.

The following excerpts are taken from *Laos: The Land and the People*, distributed by the Lutheran Immigration and Refugee Services.[25]

Values and Patterns of Living

The Lao value system derives from several different cultural traditions and shows the influences of Brahmanism and Theravada Buddhism.

The first set of values are Brahmanical, oriented toward a system of fixed classes with ascribed status and important rank distinctions. Each person has a definite place in the social order and a clearly prescribed role.

The second set of values is influenced by Theravada Buddhism. The basic concepts are the unity of all life and the ultimate spiritual perfectibility and equality of all humankind. The concepts also stress the acceptance of the secular social order, religious detachment from worldly affairs, the individual's responsibility for his or her own status in life, and the possibility of altering one's status through a combination of individual merit and reincarnation.

A third set of values derives from the French presence, which has penetrated Lao society through government education and the way of thinking. The tradition places a high value on the ability to raise one's status in life through the direct and practical means of secular education and economic advancement. It stresses active rather than passive aspects of achievement and the accumulation of material wealth to achieve both personal and social ends. This tradition is strongest among the civil servants and the upper class, who served in the previous French Administration of Laos.

Other values, those of the Chinese and those of various groups with whom the Lao have had contact over the last 2,700 years also are present.

> *"Our children have no ideas about our Catholic faith. They do not know what God is all about. We look for some CCD teachers or bible teachers to teach our children about religion."*
>
> **A Laotian parent**

Social Relationships

Lao prefer to have social relationships clearly defined so that each person has a distinct status and a prescribed role. There is security in thus knowing precisely where an individual stands, what is expected of him and others, what he and others can and cannot do. The rules of etiquette between people of different status and rank are carefully spelled out, and every status and rank has its appropriate and circumscribed roles for every situation.

The Family

The family usually lives in a closely knit unit. It is usual and normal to see grandparents sharing the same house with their married children or married grandchildren. Filial piety is less a compulsive moral obligation than the respect for one's elders expected of everyone. Buddhist teaching stresses deference to the wishes of an elder and is still the dominant influence on a young Lao's behavior. The father, usually a breadwinner, remains normally the most powerful head of the family, has authority over all family members and makes decisions on major affairs. The Lao woman occupies a key position in the household, and in many ways the prosperity, well-being and development of the family as a unit depends upon her. Her ethical influence over the younger minds is very important. In the realm of family activities, the wife stands on an equal footing with her husband—in some matters she surpasses him in initiative. Generally, it is the wife who is the treasurer, controlling the purse strings and budgeting the family assets. Lao children are treated affectionately but not fussed over and are encouraged to care for themselves from an early age.

Personal Conduct

The Lao believe that the individual should be continually attuned to the Buddhist code of personal conduct. Nonviolence is another important precept, and crimes of violence are extremely rare. In general, temperance, diligence, thrift and self-discipline are stressed.

Hospitality

Guests are always welcome, no matter how inconvenient their presence might be. Invitations are not customary for casual visits. People just visit as the spirit moves them. Displays of anger are considered rude. Confrontation is avoided lest another's feelings be injured. The indirect approach is used in matters of controversy. Generally, the Lao do not verbalize or physically show their feelings in the same way that Americans do. A thank you is likely to take the form of a slight bow, smile, and hands pressed together in front of the chest. This pressing together of the hands is known as a "wai." It is also the form of greeting, although in contacts with Americans, Lao are more likely to use the hand-shake which they know is customary among Americans.

Religion

Theravada Buddhism is the dominant religion in Laos, adhered to by nearly 90 percent of the ethnic Lao population. Most Lao are superstitious, and their supernatural traditions have deep historical roots. The supernatural traditions combine animism, sorcery, naturalism and magical rites.

The following excerpts are taken from *History of the Evangelization of Laos*, by Father Louis S. Leduc, M.E.P.[26]

Giovanni Leira, an Italian Jesuit, was in Vientiane around 1630. It was recorded that the receptivity of the Laotians to the Gospel moved Louis Laneau, the first vicar apostolic of Siam (1673-96), to send missionaries into Laos and to compose "Instructions aux missionnaires du Laos." It was discontinued because of a revolution in Thailand but was revived again in the late 19th century. In 1880, Bishop Vey, the Apostolic Vicar of Bangkok, sent two missionaries, Father Prod'homme and Father Xavier Guego, to the northeast of Thailand and Laos. The two arrived in Oubone in April, 1881 and set up a Catholic center. Evangelization started in a small way with the buying back of slaves. The King of Thailand had just proclaimed the end of slavery and wanted to free the slaves. The news of the possibility of being bought back spread rapidly and more and more slaves arrived. In order to stay under the priests' protection and also to thank them, the slaves became Catholic.

Between 1885 and 1889, the evangelization effort continued with exploratory trips to Nakhonphanom, Thakhek and Sakolnakhon. The missionaries traveled to the left bank of the Mekhong River in Laos. It was in Khamkeum, to the north of Nongseng, that the evangelization of Laos began. The first minor seminary was opened in Dondone, an island on the river between Nongseng and Thakhek, in 1891. The "mission of Laos" was erected as Vicariat Apostolique in 1889.

During the next 100 years, that one "mission of Laos" developed into eight dioceses in Laos and northeast Thailand. Each local diocese was blessed with native clergy, religious sisters, and catechists.

"We are ordinary farm people. I was drafted to serve in the army. I was injured in battle. While I was in a hospital, a priest and a catechist came to visit me. I was moved by their visit and the story of the bible. I was baptized on Christmas Day in 1962. I went on to study the bible and nursing. The challenges in this country are English language, finding a job, and poverty. The Catholic school is too expensive for us. My recommendation is that our faith in Jesus, the Church and the bible are more important than money. We need to help each other because refugees in the U.S.A. are like children, need to learn to walk, to hold our hands and to lead our ways."

A Hmong deacon and parent

The following excerpts are taken from *Evangelization of Hmong People in Laos: 1950-1975*, by Rev. Daniel E. Taillez, OMI.[27]

In 1950, Bishop Etienne Loosdregt appointed Father Yves Bertrais to minister to the Hmong people in Kiou Kacham in the Province of Louang Prabang. It took some time for several Hmong families to decide to become Catholic. Finally, in 1954, the first Hmong baptism was performed. At that time, one American Oblate and two French Oblates began learning the Hmong language.

In 1959-60, several Italian Oblates assumed the ministry to the Hmong in the Apostolic Vicariate of Louang Prabang. Fathers Bertrais, Bouchard, Charrier and Rancoeur moved to the provinces of Sam Neua and Xieng Khouang.

At the beginning of 1961, no foreign missionary was allowed to stay in Sam Neua. Due to the fact that the foreign missionaries could not stay any longer in the mountain areas in the northern provinces of Laos, two training centers for lay catechists were launched, one in Louang Prabang and one in Vientiane. In Vientiane, after four years of intensive training, Hmong catechists were appointed to minister to their own people in the remote areas where the Hmong were living. After a two year probation, catechists returned to the center in Vientiane for two more years. In sum, they received training for six full years.

Indeed, we felt quite privileged to let them be the first apostles of their own brothers and sisters. Year after year, we experienced many things; the Hmong catechists took their ministry very seriously. Their people respected them and considered them as the religious leaders.

Because of the ministry of the Hmong catechists in the northern provinces of Laos, many small Catholic communities started in many areas. A priest visited them only once a month. In 1975, throughout northern Laos, there were as many as 3,000 Hmong Catholics.

Indeed, we would not have been able to spread the Gospel to the Hmong people without the catechists. They were precious auxiliaries. We were working closely together. And we were quite grateful to the Lord because of their zeal and their commitment to the cause of the Gospel.

Between 1960 to 1975, an Italian Oblate brother plus a dozen priests, both of the Paris Foreign Mission Society and the Oblates were killed. May their lives be the seed for a future harvest.

In May, 1975 we felt sorry to have to leave Laos and abandon that field where we worked for so many years. It is useless to lament over a situation beyond our control. Let us simply be confident that some day the True Liberator will let His peace shine again upon that Kingdom of a million elephants and the white parasol.

The following excerpts are taken from *Perspective on a Cross-Cultural Problem—Getting to Know the Vietnamese*, distributed by the National Indochinese Clearing House, Center for Applied Linguistics.[28]

Vietnamese through the Eyes of Vietnamese

The following are English translations of excerpts from the book *Nguoi Viet, Dat Viet (Vietnamese People, Vietnamese Land)* by Cuu-Long-Giang and Toan-Anh, Nam Chi Tung Thu Publishers, Saigon, 1967.

Vietnamese are an intelligent people. They possess a keen sense of observation which gives them the ability to grasp things quickly; it also gives them a tendency to imitate others.

Vietnamese have a high regard for morality and uphold the five Confucian virtues of humanity, righteousness, propriety, wisdom, and faithfulness as guides for their daily conduct. They love book-study and have avid minds.

Ordinarily giving an appearance of being shy and afraid, they value peace and harmony in all relations. However, when they are faced with danger, or are on the battlefield, they display great bravery and know how to maintain discipline, giving death itself as much weight as an airborne thistledown. Often motivated by compassion for others, they have a strong sense of gratitude.

A most admirable trait in the Vietnamese, however, is the love they have for their country....

This rare description of the Vietnamese character by two Vietnamese cultural historians, interesting as it might be, gives us only a quick glimpse of what Vietnamese are like. The brief description will have to be elaborated on and complemented by other sources before a balanced and useful picture can emerge.

Other major characteristics of the Vietnamese people include a combination of thrift, industriousness, patience, determination and an endurance that allows a Vietnamese farmer to plough his field all day under the hot sun, walking slowly behind his water-buffalo, ankle-deep in the mud of the rice paddy. "Tanh can cu" is the quiet willingness to do things the hard way when the hard way is the only way possible.

"Tanh hieu hoc"—the love of learning which the Vietnamese talk about—is actually a traditional, deep, and almost subconscious respect for the learned and their learning. American educators familiar with education programs in Vietnam have often observed that the Vietnamese child's style of learning tends to be passive rather than active. The child relies more on listening, watching, and imitating than on experimenting, trying things out, and generally discovering things for himself or herself. Vietnamese students tend to be hard-working, and to give their teachers more respect than do their American counterparts.

The Vietnamese have a heart-oriented culture; this characteristic means much more than the superficial appearance of sensitive emotionalism or subtle sentimentalism. On a philosophical level, it means a characteristic and pervading humanism that permeates and gives distinctiveness to the whole culture. Vietnamese are more interested in how people feel, react, and transact than in how their physical environment operates. Their thinking is directed toward morals, ethics, and the formulation of rules of conduct rather than toward the discovery of laws and principles that govern nature.

For the Vietnamese in their various everyday encounters, "propriety" means the almost subconscious and reflex-like application of tacit rules of decorum which are translated into behaviors characteristically Vietnamese. They are formal in their interpersonal relations. They appear to be protocol-minded and to place a value on decorum, etiquette and ceremony. The formality is deeply rooted in the Vietnamese culture seen as an aspect of the Confucian concept of "le" or "propriety," one of the five constant virtues that "guide the thoughts, deeds and words of the superior man." The Vietnamese word for politeness, "le phep," literally means "rules of propriety."

American social scientist Abraham M. Hirsh, an expert in cross-cultural communication and an astute observer of the Vietnamese value system, thinks that the Vietnamese use what he terms a "pluralistic approach to life-manship," with a strong inclination for eclectic adaptations. There is an element here that is common to hundreds of other cases observed both in Vietnam and in the United States. And that is the ability of the Vietnamese to hold more than one religious belief, to espouse more than one ideal, accept more than one solution to a problem, attempt more than one course of action, and generally tolerate more than one absolute standard for anything. In philosophical terms, the inclination to follow more than one path has been associated with eclecticism. Their tendency to seek the other alternatives, the working combination, has been labeled syncretism. Syncretism requires an ability to reconcile opposing principles and practices in an effort to make them work harmoniously. Thus, the Vietnamese syncretism is seen to stem from a harmony-orientation.

Many observers feel that the need for a sense of permanence in life is strong in the Vietnamese. Customs, traditions change slowly with them. The sense of permanence can also be seen in the Vietnamese view of death. A link between the dead and the living is maintained by way of the annual family rituals of commemoration held for each deceased family member. On the day of each commemoration, an actual meal — usually more elaborate than an ordinary family meal — is prepared and served on the family altar, where incense and aromatic joss sticks are burned. With a cultural clock "walking" rather than "running," a Vietnamese is more accustomed to a day that is less hurried than an American's day.

In seeking to understand the Vietnamese, we again call attention to the little Vietnamese saying:

"Di Lau moi biet duong dai, O lau moi biet nguoi phai chang."

"Just as the length of a road is known only by actually traveling on it, the qualities of a man are known only by living with him for a long time."

Religion in Vietnam

As in other Asian nations, Buddhism is the predominant religion in Vietnam, appearing in the form of the Mahayana school. This religion was introduced when Vietnam was dominated by China in the second century. It eventually became the state religion under the Ly Dynasty (1010-1214).[29] Even though Buddhism lost its influence in the Tran Dynasty (1225-1440), it still remains the most practiced religion in the country.

Besides Buddhism, Confucianism and Taoism are influential in Vietnam. Confucianism is not a religion in its accepted meaning of the word, but rather a religious and social philosophy of life. "Confucianism advocates a code of social behavior that people ought to observe so as to live in harmony in society and attain happiness in individual life."[30] Taoism is also a religious philosophy. It directs humans to have harmony with others, and with the environment. "To achieve this harmony, all forms of confrontation should be avoided. The virtues of simplicity, patience, and self-contentment must be observed. By non-action and keeping away from human strife and cravings, one can reach harmony with oneself, other people, and the universe. Reason and knowledge cannot lead one to the right path (Tao) which can be reached only by inward probing and quiet meditation."[31]

> "*The church opened her arm to us when we arrived in this country. We lost everything in 1975. Yet, this helps me to prioritize my values and try to cope with the adaptation in this country.*"
>
> **A Vietnamese community leader**

Christianity entered Vietnam in the sixteenth century through the Portuguese, Spanish and French missionaries. Through evangelization and education, Christianity began to spread rapidly. However, it faced severe persecution under the Nguyen Dynasty, especially under kings Minh-Mang, Thieu Tri, and Tu-Duc. The French utilized the persecution of Christians as a pretext for establishing domination in the second half of the nineteenth century. Before the fall of Saigon in 1975, even representing a very small number of the total population, the Catholics played an important role in the political life in Vietnam.[32]

The Refugees from Indochina into the United States (1975-1990)

A refugee, by the definition according to the Immigration and Nationality Act, means "any person who is outside of his or her country, and is unable to or unwilling to return to, and is unable or unwilling to avail himself or herself of the protection of that country because of persecution or a well-founded fear of persecution on account of race, religion, nationality, membership in a particular social group, or political opinion...."[33] From 1975 to 1989, 930,158 Indochinese refugees entered the United States. This number included refugees admitted through the Orderly Departure Program (ODP) from Vietnam.[34] The refugees from Cambodia, Laos and Vietnam were resettled throughout the country.

Most of these people could confirm that the refugee experience is a traumatic experience. The Vietnamese refugees came to the United States by airlift in the beginning. Later they came by boats and by land. The refugees from Laos went across the Mekhong River to refugee camps in Thailand. The Cambodian refugees also had to endure hardship in the jungles before they reached the Thai refugee camps. Some fifteen years after Indochina shifted to communist rule, Indochinese refugees are still seeking a place to live in the United States.

The Cambodian, Laotian and Vietnamese Catholic Communities in the United States

Between 1975 and 1989, 144,745 Cambodian refugees were resettled in the United States.[35] It is estimated that 1,100 of these Cambodians are Catholic.[36] Most of the Cambodian Catholics are scattered across the country in places such as Lowell, Massachusetts; Long Beach, California; and Annandale, Virginia. To address the pastoral care of the Cambodian Catholics resettled all over the country, the Bishop Salas Cambodian Catholic Center was established as a resource center and to coordinate the itinerant ministry for the Cambodian Catholics. Father Rogatien Rondineau, a French missionary from Cambodia, is the Director of this center.[37] Only a few priests can communicate in Khmer, the language of Cambodia.

In 1975, after the Pathet Lao had taken power in Laos, many groups that supported the United States had to flee the country. By the end of 1989, 204,800 refugees from Laos had been admitted to the United States.[38] U.S. Department of State records indicate that more than 72,000 came from Highland Laos.[39] Many of the Lao Catholic population are among these refugees.

The Catholic Lao have been resettled all across the country, and many Hmong and Laotian Catholic communities have been established. According to the survey study of the *Apostolate Profile of the Catholic Communities of the Cambodian, Hmong, Kmhmu and Laotian People* by the Office for the Pastoral Care of Migrants and Refugees:

A Catholic community refers to the Catholic population of an area. Each community can be centered around a diocese, a center or a local parish. None of these groups has its own parish, as might have been the case when 'national' parishes were more readily established. Some do have the liturgy in their own languages as they share the physical plant with an American parish. The number of Catholics in each community varies. In some larger communities, the numbers of people can range from 500-900 people. In other communities, the numbers are much smaller: only 7, 15, 30 or 70 people. The greater the Catholic population in an area, the more likely services such as a Pastoral Center, ministers who can communicate in that particular ethnic group's language, or more extensive outreach to refugees can be found."[40]

The apostolates to the Hmong, Cambodians, Kmhmu and Laotians require a national perspective and coordination. The size and separation of the refugee communities are the two main reasons the National Pastoral Centers were established. Another reason is the small number of priests and sisters capable of communicating in these languages. Of the three apostolates, only one Laotian native priest and three Laotian sisters are resettled in this country. There are three centers for the Hmong Apostolate, including the East Coast Ministry to the Hmong in Providence, Rhode Island; the Hmong Catholic Center in St. Paul, Minnesota; and the Asian Ministry Office—Hmong Center in Fresno, California. The center for the Cambodians is the Bishop Salas Cambodian Pastoral Center located in Annandale, Virginia. The Laotian Pastoral Center is located in Fort Worth, Texas.

These centers provide national coordination of pastoral models that respond to the spiritual needs of the people. They coordinate itinerant and team mission ministry in different communities throughout the country. They also produce catechetical, spiritual and liturgical materials in their own languages. The National Pastoral Centers are the resource centers for these particular ethnic apostolates."[41]

Pastoral Care of Vietnamese Catholics in the United States, A Preliminary Report. This report was prepared by the Office for Pastoral Care of Migrants and Refugees, USCC.[42]

Between 1975 and the end of 1989, more than half a million Vietnamese refugees had been admitted into the United States. It is estimated that more than 150,000 are Catholics, with large concentrations in Louisiana, Texas, California (Orange County, San Jose), Washington (Seattle), Northern Virginia and generally in the South and West.

More than 130 Vietnamese Catholic communities and Catholic Vietnamese Unions are actively functioning in 28 dioceses throughout the United States. Among these, ten ethnic and personal parishes have been decreed and established by the bishops in various states from Virginia to Nebraska. Such personal parishes enjoy the canonical status of a diocesan parish and the Vietnamese pastor is appointed by the local bishop. These parishes and communities are mostly autonomous and fulfill their own needs according to their local situation. They depend on the leadership of the individual chaplain or pastor and on the degree of involvement and know-how of the elected representatives of the Vietnamese community. Their activities are limited to Sunday liturgy, some catechism, and a few special cultural events during the course of the year, for example, Christmas, Vietnamese Tet (New Year), and feasts of the Vietnamese Blessed Martyrs.

In areas of Vietnamese concentration, diocesan programs for Vietnamese have been encouraged. Diocesan coordination offices or programs for Vietnamese language ministry have been established in many dioceses. In the Archdiocese of New Orleans the Vietnamese Apostolate was established in 1975, and has a team of five priests to provide pastoral care to the large numbers of Catholic refugees. Another diocesan coordination program was initiated by the Diocese of Orange, California. The Vietnamese Catholic Center with a team of 6 priests and a community of the Lovers of the Holy Cross of Phat Diem Sisters take care of the ministry of Sacraments and religious education for 15,000 people resettled in Orange County. The diocese of Portland, Oregon established a multi-cultural center, The Southeast Asian Vicariate, to serve the pastoral needs of about 4,000 Catholic Indochinese refugees. There are other programs for the pastoral care of Vietnamese coordinated on the diocesan level in San Jose, Philadelphia, Harrisburg, San Diego, Seattle, Baltimore, and Denver, to name a few. Each of these communities is privileged to have a full-time Vietnamese priest assigned by the Ordinary to this area of service, and they call themselves Community of Vietnamese Catholics of the specific diocese where they reside. Each communitiy is a single Catholic organization with pastoral programs accountable to the local bishop.

> *"The loneliness and the trauma will stay with us for a long time. Indeed our faith will provide us with reasons-of-being, reasons of hope. As a matter of fact our faith has to enlighten our daily life."*
> **A Hmong deacon and parent**

Other Pastoral Resources and Programs are the following:

(1) In the Midwest, the Congregation of the Mother Co-Redemptrix (CMC) has opened its Provincial House in Carthage, Missouri to thousands of pilgrims who come to celebrate Marian Day, a weekend festival of religious and cultural activities that include a Pontifical Mass, liturgy for various groups, a procession in honor of Mary and the Vietnamese Blessed Martyrs, prayer group meetings, adoration of the Blessed Sacrament, reconciliation services and cultural performances. This Marian Day celebration has become an annual pilgrimage for the Vietnamese since 1978.

(2) In the East, the Vietnamese Catholics are scattered in small numbers and tend to be assimilated into local English speaking parishes. No Vietnamese pastoral center has been established, except the personal parishes in Arlington, Richmond, and Washington, D.C. dioceses.

(3) Vietnamese youth are a special concern for pastoral care. From the beginning,

priests and community leaders, who were well aware of the many urgent problems and serious crises encountered by young refugees, made many attempts to bring together the youth in retreats to instruct, to guide and to share problems and convictions in order to help them cope with the new culture and a very different environment. In 1982, Father Julien Elizalde Thanh, SJ, was assigned by his superior to come to the United States from Manila to devote himself full-time to preaching retreats to large groups of Vietnamese youth. He and his team spent six months traveling through the United States and Canada, using the Spiritual Exercises of the Jesuits to help Vietnamese young people rediscover the meaning and purpose of life. Because there are many requests from various Vietnamese communities throughout the country, Father Elizalde and his team must schedule retreats all year long to meet the needs of the youth. A follow-up program was also established. Christian Life Communities (CLC) have been started in many locations to sustain the spiritual commitments of young Vietnamese.

(4) The Renew Program has been introduced to a number of Vietnamese communities in New Orleans, Houston, Seattle, and San Jose by Father Joachim Le Quang Hien of Spokane.

(5) Along with the Cursillo Movement, which holds annual retreats in Orange County and New Orleans, many pious groups such as the Legion of Mary and the Third Order of Saint Francis are active on the West Coast and in the southern part of the United States.

There is a large number of Vietnamese priests, religious and seminarians in the United States. A study by the Center for Applied Research in the Apostolate (CARA), "A Commentary on Seminary Priesthood: Enrollment Statistics for 1989—Part I & II," shows the number of Asian seminarians. Among the various Asian Catholic communities, Vietnamese vocations outnumber those of other Asian communities. The data on Vietnamese vocations nationally show the following: 108 Vietnamese in seminary high schools; 127 Vietnamese in seminary colleges; and 107 Vietnamese in seminary theologates.[43]

Today, at the national level, the coordination of the Vietnamese Apostolate is carried out by the National Conference of Catholic Bishops through the Office for the Pastoral Care of Migrants and Refugees, which established the National Pastoral Center for the Vietnamese Apostolate in 1989.

Conclusion

Some 15 years after Indochina fell to communism, Indochinese refugees continue to flee their homelands. Hundreds of thousands of refugees are still in the camps in Hong Kong, the Philippines, Thailand and Malaysia. Those who have made it to the United States brought with them diverse backgrounds. Unlike other Asian immigrants, these people are truly uprooted. "The refugees are like the homeless people," lamented one of them. "They have no place they can call their own. They feel no sense of belonging to this land." In Texas, another refugee wrote:

> In the obscurity of the night, a refugee cries
> His tear of woe flooded on his eyes
> He sobs for homeless life,
> the uncertainty of tomorrow....[44]

Footnotes

1. *The Peoples and Cultures of Cambodia, Laos, and Vietnam*, Center for Applied Linguistics, Washington, DC, p. 2.
2. *Ibid.*, p. 3.
3. Mary Bower Wright, "Indochinese," *Harvard Encyclopedia of American Ethnic Groups*, Stephan Thernstrom, ed., The Belknap Press of Harvard University Press, Cambridge, MA, 1980, p. 508.
4. Huynh Dinh Te, "Introduction to Vietnamese Culture," *Introduction to Cambodian Culture, Laos Culturally Speaking, Introduction to Vietnamese Culture*, Multifunctional Resource Center, San Diego, CA, 1989, p. 179.
5. Wright, "Indochinese," p. 509.
6. *Ibid.*
7. Ronald Takaki, *Strangers from a Different Shore, A History of Asian Americans*, Little, Brown and Company, Boston, MA, 1989, p. 449.
8. *Refugee Reports*, A News Service of the U.S. Committee for Refugees, Vol.X, no. 12, December 29, 1989, p. 9.
9. Sun-Him Chhim, "Introduction to Cambodian Culture," *Introduction to Cambodian Culture, Laos Culturally Speaking, Introduction to Vietnamese Culture*, pp. 9-10.
10. *Ibid.*, p. 11.
11. *Ibid.*, p. 12.
12. *Ibid.*, p. 13.
13. *Ibid.*, p. 15.
14. *Ibid.*, pp. 17-19.
15. *The Peoples and Cultures of Cambodia, Laos, and Vietnam*, p. 25.
16. *Ibid.*
17. *Ibid.*
18. Takaki, *Strangers from a Different Shore*, p. 462.
19. *Profiles of the Highland Lao Communities in the United States*, Doua Yang and David North, prepared for the U.S. Department of Health and Human Services, Washington, DC, November 1988, p. 6.
20. Huynh Dinh Te, "Introduction to Vietnamese Culture," p. 139.
21. *Ibid.*, p. 140.
22. *Ibid.*
23. Used with permission. *Cambodia: The Land and Its People*, produced by Lutheran Immigration and Refugee Service, New York, revised 1983, pp. 2-5.
24. Used with permission. Rev. Rogatien Rondineau, MEP, "Evangelization in

Cambodia," *Proceedings of the First Meeting of the Cambodian, Hmong and Laotian Apostolate in the Catholic Church in the United States*, sponsored by NCCB, Bishops' Committee on Migration and Tourism, Pastoral Care of Migrants and Refugees, Washington, DC, 1985, pp. 6-7.

25. Used with permission. *Laos, the Land and the People*, prepared by the Lutheran Immigration and Refugee Services, a department of the Division of Mission and Ministry of the Lutheran Council in the U.S.A., New York, revised 1987, pp. 15-21.

26. Used with permission. Rev. Louis S. Leduc, MEP., "History of the Evangelization of Laos," *Proceedings of the First Meeting of the Cambodian, Hmong and Laotian Apostolate in the Catholic Church in the United States*, sponsored by NCCB, Bishops' Committee on Migration and Tourism, Pastoral Care of Migrants and Refugees, Washington, DC, 1985, pp. 10-11.

27. Used with permission. Rev. Daniel E. Taillez, OMI., "Evangelization of Hmong People in Laos: 1950-1975," *Proceedings of the First Meeting of the Cambodian, Hmong and Laotian Apostolate in the Catholic Church in the United States*, sponsored by NCCB, Bishops' Committee on Migration and Tourism, Pastoral Care of Migrants and Refugees, Washington, DC, 1985, pp. 8-9.

28. Used with permission. *History and Culture of Vietnam: an Introduction*, prepared by Lutheran Immigration and Refugee Service. This information is condensed from *A Manual for Indochinese Refugee Education, 1976-1977*, prepared by the Center for Applied Linguistics, Washington, DC, 1981, pp. 2-21.

29. Huyenh Dinh Te, "Introduction to Vietnamese Culture," p. 209.

30. *Ibid.*, p. 210.

31. *Ibid.*, p. 211.

32. *Ibid.*, p. 212.

33. Bari Chase, Juliet Turner, Cindy Wagner, managing editors, *Bender's Immigration and Nationality Act Pamphlet*, New York, 1989, p. 24.

34. *Refugee Reports*, p. 9.

35. *Refugee Reports*, p. 10.

36. *Apostolate Profile of the Catholic Communities of the Cambodian, Hmong, Kmhmu, and Laotian People*, prepared by USCC, Migration and Refugee Services, Office for the Pastoral Care of Migrants and Refugees (Washington, D.C., 1989), p. 2.

37. *Ibid.*, appendix 2.

38. *Refugee Reports*, p. 10.

39. *Profiles of the Highland Lao Communities in the United States*, p. 7.

40. *Apostolate Profiles of the Catholic Communities of the Cambodian, Hmong, Kmhmu and Laotian People*, p. 2.

41. *Ibid.*, p. 20.

42. This report has been prepared by the Office of the Pastoral Care of Migrants and Refugees, staff-service on the National Conference of Catholic Bishops' Committee on Migration and Tourism, with the assistance of Rev. Joseph Thuy, Washington, DC, 1985.

43. *CARA Seminary Forum*, "A Commentary on Seminary Priesthood, Enrollment

Statistics for 1989 - Part I & II," vol.16-17, nos.1-4 (1989).
    44. Takaki, *Strangers from a Different Shore*, p. 471.

Acknowledgements

The sections on *The Peoples, Cultures and Religions of Cambodia, Laos, and Vietnam* are condensed from the following:

Cambodia: The Land and Its People, produced by the Lutheran Immigration and Refugee Service, New York, 1983.

Laos: The Land and the People, prepared by the Lutheran Immigration and Refugee Services, New York, 1987.

History and Culture of Vietnam: An Introduction, prepared by the Lutheran Immigration and Refugee Services, 1986. This information is condensed from *A Manual for Indochinese Refugee Education, 1976-1977*, prepared by Center for Applied Linguistics, Washington, DC, 1981.

Rev. Rogatien Rondineau, MEP., "Evangelization in Cambodia," *Proceedings of the First Meeting of the Cambodian, Hmong and Laotian Apostolate in the Catholic Church in the United States*, sponsored by NCCB, Bishops' Committee on Migration and Tourism, Pastoral Care of Migrants and Refugees, Washington, DC, 1985.

Rev. Louis S. Leduc, MEP., "History of the Evangelization of Laos," *Proceedings of the First Meeting of the Cambodian, Hmong and Laotian Apostolate in the Catholic Church in the United States*, sponsored by NCCB, Bishops' Committee on Migration and Tourism, Pastoral Care of Migrants and Refugees, Washington, DC, 1985.

Rev. Daniel E. Taillez, OMI., "Evangelization of Hmong People in Laos: 1950-1975," *Proceedings of the First Meeting of the Cambodian, Hmong and Laotian Apostolate in the Catholic Church in the United States*, sponsored by NCCB, Bishops' Committee on Migration and Tourism, Pastoral Care of Migrants and Refugees, Washington, DC, 1985.

CHAPTER II

Demographics

Asian Populations

With the change in immigration policies in 1965, the Asian community has been growing rapidly. By 1987, over 40% of all immigrants who came to the United States were from Asia. For instance, since 1960 more immigrants have come to the United States from the Philippines than from all other countries except Mexico.

The following census data illustrate the beginnings and growth of the Asian American population in the U.S.:

TOTAL U.S. AND ASIAN AMERICAN POPULATION
1900-1980

Census year	Total U.S.	Total Asian
1900	76,212,168	204,462
1910	92,228,531	249,926
1920	106,021,568	332,432
1930	123,202,660	489,326
1940	132,165,129	489,984
1950	151,325,798	599,091
1960	179,323,175	877,934
1970	203,211,926	1,429,562
1980	226,545,805	3,466,421

Source: "Asian Americans: Growth, Change & Diversity," *Population Bulletin*, 1985.

The arrival of Asian Americans began with the recruitment of Chinese to work in California's gold mines in the mid-nineteenth century. Thousands followed, building the transcontinental railroads. Japanese workers replaced the Chinese when Congress passed the Chinese Exclusion Act. By 1900, 204,462 Asians including 119,000 Chinese and 86,000 Japanese were counted by the census. For the first time this count included Hawaii which was annexed in 1898. By 1930, the Asian populations had more than doubled to almost half a million persons, and by 1970 they comprised about 1.5 million. During the seventies they increased by 141% (Black population increase was 17%; Hispanic population 39%) and in 1985 it is estimated that the Asian population was 5.2 million, or about 2.1% of the total population.

During the 1980s the Asian population was projected to grow by 58% or 5.9 million, and during 1990s they will continue to increase by another 38% or 8.1 million. Beginning as a small minority, by the middle of the next century they will be as large a minority as Hispanics are now.

ASIAN POPULATION 1980, 1985

	1980		1985	
	Number	Percent	Number	Percent
Chinese	812,000	23%	1,079,000	21%
Filipino	782,000	23%	1,051,000	20%
Japanese	716,000	21%	766,000	15%
Asian Indian	387,000	11%	626,000	10%
Korean	357,000	10%	542,000	11%
Vietnamese	245,000	7%	634,000	12%

Source: "Asian Americans: Growth, Change and Diversity," *Population Bulletin*, 1985.

ASIAN POPULATION, 1980-2020
(in thousands)

	Chinese	Asian Indian	Japanese	Korean	Filipino	Vietnamese	Other Asian
1980	812	387	716	357	782	245	166
1990	1,124	622	833	711	1,269	525	706
2000	1,440	875	936	1,092	1,783	830	1,338

ASIAN POPULATION, 1980 - 2020
(in thousands)

	1980		1990		2000		2010		2020	
	#	%	#	%	#	%	#	%	#	%
Chinese	812	23%	1,124	22%	1,440	21%	1,749	20%	2,033	19%
Filipino	782	23%	1,269	25%	1,783	26%	2,296	26%	2,802	26%
Japanese	716	21%	833	16%	936	13%	1,025	11%	1,078	10%
Asian Indian	387	11%	622	12%	875	13%	1,128	13%	1,376	13%
Korean	357	10%	711	14%	1,092	15%	1,479	17%	1,874	18%
Vietnamese	245	7%	525	11%	830	12%	1,139	13%	1,456	14%
TOTALS for above groups	3.3 M		5.1 M		6.9 M		8.8 M		10.6 M	

Source: *American Demographics*, "The Fastest Growing Minority," May 1985.

The six largest groups are of Asian peoples are Chinese, Filipino, Japanese, Asian Indian, Korean and Vietnamese. Our study is concerned with these six groups and two additional Indochinese groups—Cambodian and Laotian. These groups include over 95% of Asian Americans in the 1980 Census. Chinese are the largest group and comprise one-fifth or 21% of all Asians. Filipinos have increased since 1980 and are 20% and Japanese 15%. The other groups each comprise close to one-tenth of the Asian population: Vietnamese 12%, Koreans 11% and Asian Indians 10%. In particular, Vietnamese have increased dramatically since 1980, and have more than doubled to nearly 650,000.

Less than half, (41%) of Asian-Americans were born in this country, but this differs among Asian groups. Close to three-fourths of Japanese were born in the U.S. as compared to 37% of the Chinese, 35% of the Filipinos and less than 10% of the Vietnamese.

Geographic Concentrations

SEVEN STATES WITH 100,000 OR MORE ASIAN AMERICANS IN 1980
(Population numbers in thousands)

Area	Total US population	Total Asian	Japanese	Chinese	Filipino	Korean	Asian Indian	Vietnamese
U.S.	226,546	3,466	716	812	782	357	387	245
Percent	100.0	100.0	100.0	100.0	100.0	100.0	100.0	100.0
California	23,668	1,247	269	326	358	103	60	85
Percent	10.4	36.0	37.5	40.1	45.8	28.7	15.4	34.8
Hawaii	965	453	240	56	132	17	1	3
Percent	0.4	13.1	33.5	6.9	16.9	4.9	0.2	1.4
New York	17,558	328	25	147	36	33	68	6
Percent	7.8	9.4	3.5	18.1	4.6	9.3	17.5	2.4
Illinois	11,427	171	18	29	44	24	37	6
Percent	5.0	4.9	2.6	3.6	5.7	6.8	9.7	2.6
Texas	14,229	130	12	27	16	14	23	28
Percent	6.3	3.7	1.7	3.3	2.0	3.9	6.0	11.3
New Jersey	7,365	108	10	23	24	13	31	3
Percent	3.3	3.1	1.4	2.9	3.1	3.7	7.9	1.2
Washington	4,132	105	27	18	26	13	4	9
Percent	1.8	3.0	3.8	2.2	3.3	3.8	1.1	3.6

Source: Bureau of the Census, *1980 Census of Population*

Geographically, Asian Americans are concentrated in five states: California, Hawaii, New York, Illinois and Texas. An estimate of the 1985 Asian population shows that zip codes with the largest number of Asians are in New York, California and Chicago, Illinois. Also, the states with zip codes where the Asian population is growing fastest are Arizona, California, Hawaii, New Mexico, and Texas.

Census Data

For the 1980 United States decennial census, three and a half million persons identified themselves as Asian. Since then two-fifths of immigrants coming to the United States were from Asia and by the middle of the next century it is anticipated that the Asian populations will be as large as the current Hispanic population.

The countries from which the six largest Asian populations come are quite different in traditions as the previous sections of this study show, and these Asian groups in the United States also vary by geographic residence and place of birth. As noted earlier, while most Asians are born abroad, a large majority of Japanese were born in the United States in contrast to only one-tenth of the Vietnamese who are among the most recent immigrants to arrive. Seven-tenths of the Asian population lives in five states: California, Hawaii, New York, Illinois and Texas, but there are also indications that Asians are settling in other areas.

Age
Asian communities are young communities. The median age is 28.4 and 6% are 65 years of age and older compared with the U.S. population with a median age of 30.0 and with 11% of the population being 65 years of age or older. Differences among the Asian groups are present. For the Japanese, the median age is 33.5; the Vietnamese are the youngest with a median age of 21.5.

Family size
The size of Asian families is large, averaging 3.8 persons. The national family size averages 3.3 persons. In the Asian communities, more young children under 18 are likely to be with both parents, and their households are more likely to include elderly as members. The median size of the family, however, is different for various groups. On an average the Vietnamese have the largest families with 5.2 members, and Asian Indians the smallest with 3.5 persons.

Income
Median family income is higher for Asian families than the U.S. at large. Their median family income is $22,700 (1980), as compared to the national median family income of $19,900 (1980). The Japanese have the highest family income averaging $27,400, and the Vietnamese the lowest income averaging $12,800.

However, the proportion of poor families is slightly higher in the Asian community (13%) than for the United States in general (12%). The presence of poverty also varies among the Asian groups. Among the Vietnamese families over one-third or

35% live in poverty; for the Japanese and Filipino families only 7% live in poverty.

The overall higher income of the Asian families also reflects the fact that Asian families have more workers. Seventeen percent of their families have three or more workers compared to 13% of U.S. families in general. Filipino families are most likely to have three or more workers - one out of five Filipino families or 22%; the Asian Indian families are least likely with less than 10% following this pattern.

Education

Respect for education is present in the traditions of all of the Asian communities and is reflected in their overall educational level both for high school and college. Nationally, two-thirds or 66% of the U.S. population are high school graduates. For all Asians, three-quarters or 75% completed their high school education. This varies among the groups. The Japanese have the highest proportion of high school graduates with 82%, and the Vietnamese the lowest with 62%. Differences are also present by gender; 79% of Asian men and 71% of Asian women graduate from high school. An exception to this pattern is the Filipino community where more women are high school graduates.

At the college level, the Asian population as a whole is well-educated. For the United States in general, one sixth or 16% are college graduates, but proportionately this is twice as high for Asians for whom one-third or 33% are college graduates. Again this varied among groups. Asian Indians have the largest proportion of college graduates, about half, and the Vietnamese the smallest, 13%.

Catholic Population

I t is difficult to gather figures accurately on numbers of Catholics in the total Asian populations worldwide. It is even more difficult to ascertain accurately the number of Catholics in the Asian population in the United States. Two sources give us some idea of Catholics from the six countries in this study: 1) Catholic population in the homeland countries and 2) the reports of the pastoral minsters serving these populations.

CATHOLICS IN ASIA (in millions)			
Country	Total Population	Christians	Catholics
China	890	1.8	1.1
Hong Kong	5	0.8	0.3
Taiwan	17	0.9	0.4
Philippines	52	49.2	41.6
Japan	118	3.5	0.4
Asian India	694	27.2	15.3
South Korea	37	11.4	1.1
North Korea	18	0.2	0.0
Vietnam	49	3.6	3.4

Source: *World Catholicism in Transition*, 1988.

The Philippines has the largest Catholic population. India has the most Catholic pastoral personnel and Japan has the highest pastoral personnel per 1,000 Catholics. Selected Catholic pastoral ministers serving these populations in the United States are in process of gathering data regarding the number of Catholic Asians in their dioceses.

References

Bouvier, Leon F. and Anthony J. Agresta, , "The Fastest Growing Minority," *American Demographics*, May, 1985.

Gannon, Thomas, SJ, ed. *World Catholicism in Transition*, 1988.

Gardner, Robert W., Bryant Robey and Peter C. Smith, "Asian Americans: Growth, Change & Diversity," *Population Bulletin*, 1985.

U.S. Department of Commerce, Bureau of the Census. *We the Asian and Pacific Islander Americans*. U.S. Government Printing Office, Washington, DC 20402, 1988.

CHAPTER III

Educational Considerations

A fundamental goal of Catholic educational institutions is to provide quality education and equality of opportunity. In spite of this altruistic purpose, however, many ethnic groups have suffered as a result of the assimilationist philosophy which equates equality with a systematic absorption into the dominant culture.

Assimilationist education often encourages one pattern of behavior commonly accepted by the majority and one distinct language and style pertinent to that particular culture. The goal of assimilationist education is to provide a mechanism for socializing immigrants and lower class students. Its symbol is the "melting pot" which suggests a single, all-embracing culture.

Schools with a multi-ethnic population and an assimilationist philosophy tend to have lower levels of educational achievement due to some students' poor self-esteem and others' negative attitudes toward their own cultural group. In such schools teachers are more inclined to blame the students for their failure. Furthermore, ethnic gangs, negative stereotyping, school evasion, vandalism and anti-social behavior easily develop.

In recent years we have been witnessing an increasing concern for the implementation of a different approach to education, that of cultural pluralism. This stresses the integration of cultural values and customs not only in the school's stated goals and objectives, but also in all aspects of school life.

Multicultural education, as opposed to assimilationist education, is a process whereby cultural behavior and cultural differences are regarded as teaching and learning tools, used to create a fair system that may ensure all students an equal chance to acquire social, academic, and spiritual skills. It is not limited to the study of ethnicity and it is not viewed only as a concern for minorities.[1]

A multicultural approach to teaching periodically searches and researches values, customs, cultural norms and gifts of its students in order to properly and effectively incorporate them into the school's formal and informal curriculum. Empathy, cultural awareness and willingness to alter and modify are basic principles of multiculturalism. Its symbol is the "mixed salad or fruit bowl" or the "mosaic picture."

Schools with a multicultural population and a multicultural approach to education often demonstrate higher levels of cooperation, integration and educational achievement. They generate a sense of belonging, equal status among students and freedom to pursue opportunities.

"Multicultural education recognizes cultural diversity as a fact of life in American society, and it affirms that this cultural diversity is a valuable resource that should be preserved and extended. It affirms that major educational institutions should strive to preserve and enhance cultural pluralism."[2]

This multicultural approach, although conceptually understood and accepted by many, has yet to gain significant status in the restructuring of present educational practices. All educators should be aware of the negative principles of the assimilationist philosophy so that they may apply the multicultural one. In the meeting of many cultures, all groups can find identity and enrichment.

The Process of Inculturation

The people being educated in Catholic schools and in all parish programs should feel "at home" with what they learn, with the matter in which they are being taught, and with the way they are being encouraged to express and live their faith. This will happen only if the religious education they are receiving is integrated with the "familiar"—with their own culture.

Since the 1977 Synod of Bishops on Catechesis, the dimension of *inculturation* has become a focal point in religious education, alerting educators to the importance of culture in the development and education of the total person.

Inculturation enables the Church to speak *with* and not only to the people of today, in a language that expresses, through signs and symbols, their genuine problems and needs. Obviously, these needs are to be considered in their totality: physical, intellectual, spiritual, material, personal, and communal.

Inculturation takes into account all these human aspects and must not be limited to the cognitive dimension. The evaluation of whether or not a program of religious education has been planned and carried out with inculturation in mind, should be extended to the affective and behavioral dimensions.

Rather than a method or approach, inculturation is an attitude of respect for and faith in God and each individual person, whoever he or she might be.

Respect comes from the awareness that the cultural roots of every individual are integral to his or her personality. Respect for these roots implies that they are not simply taken for granted, but that they are recognized as a particular aspect of the gift of life given by God to the person. To get to know and teach anyone in an integral way, it is imperative that his or her cultural roots be taken into consideration.

Faith asserts that everything that is good and true has its source in God; and it is a fact that, no matter how "primitive" and "under-developed" a culture might seem in the eyes of "modern" society, it has elements of goodness and truth. These elements are, therefore, signs of God's salvific presence. Faith gives the Christian educator the awareness that God, Creator and Father of all, is actively engaged in every aspect of the human development of each individual person.

Inculturation is, in fact, the discovery of Gospel values already contained in and lived in any given culture, whether or not the people themselves are aware of the Christian dimension in their lives. It is the role of the religious educator to point these values out, affirm them and explicitly associate them with Christ.

Religious education and catechetical programs have to meet the challenge of an existential reality; there is no one culture which, to the exclusion of others, is capable of fully understanding and assimilating the meaning of God's revelation, and adequately expressing the human response to God's invitation to every human being, "to be saved and come to the knowledge of truth" (Timothy 2:4). Therefore, aware of the enrichment every culture can bring a deeper Christian faith and a more Catholic formation, catechesis now stresses more and more the important role of inculturation.

On the other hand, the cultural root paradigm which molds and dictates the attitudes, customs, actions and reactions of individuals in a particular society, may not always reflect Christian values. All cultures, therefore, must be "tested", so that only those aspects must be purified. Thus, genuine inculturation calls for a double discernment:

- to discover the goodness already inherent in a given cultural characteristic or custom, in order to affirm it;
- to detect whatever is evil or destructive, in order to help eradicate it.

Enculturation and Acculturation

The Catholic educator, sensitive to the value of inculturation must be involved in facilitating both the enculturation and acculturation of Asians and other ethnic groups.

Enculturation is the process by which every individual from the time of conception is molded by the culture of his or her people. Even though culture is integral to the mentality and value system of generations, and its root paradigm goes deeper than a few generations of people, it is usually the extended family that provides the environment where the child absorbs and learns the language, customs, rituals, and beliefs peculiar to its culture.

Tragically, when families migrate and are uprooted from their native country, they can no longer provide for their growing children the same environment where cultural values can be experienced and appreciated. This is especially so when immigrants are made to feel "inferior" and unwanted. They become "ashamed" of their ethnicity, language, customs and religiosity and in many ways try to hide it. Religious educators should be ready to help immigrants recall, understand and explain to their children the values of their customs and especially the religious symbols underlying what they do.

Acculturation is the sociological tendency to accommodate to a new culture. As immigrants are confronted with a multiplicity of demands and pressure to survive, they gradually tend to adopt the life style of American society. This tendency has a two-fold danger: that of stifling their cultural values and characteristics (so that they are not passed on to their children), and that of imitating some of the evil aspects of a materialistic society. This is a danger that affects everyone in the Church.

The Catholic educator responds to these two realities by encouraging and facilitating the on-going transmission of culture—*enculturation*, and by helping Asians to learn from and adopt the values of the "new" American culture in which they now live, while recognizing and rejecting its evil aspects—*acculturation*.

This requires knowledge and appreciation of both the cultural values of the particular ethnic groups and the demands of the multicultural society where they have to live and work. It requires also some degree of compromise.

For instance, Asians have a strong sense of family. In order to help young Asians experience these values (enculturation), school and parish programs should provide opportunities for Asian families to come together to celebrate their special feast days, inviting all members of the extended families to participate. Everyone is encouraged to prepare and bring their own special food and play their typical music. This responds to a genuine need in their culture.

Thus, *enculturation* and *acculturation* are not contradictory by complementary to *inculturation*, and of real value to Catholic education in a multicultural society.

Because church educators and ministers recognize the Asian presence as valuable and desirable, the following recommendations are given in order to foster a more Christian integration.

Catholic Centers for Enculturation and Acculturation

Church/Parish

1) Asians should not perceive the church as an "Americanizing agency," but as the sign and instrument of intimate union with God and with all people regardless of their ethnic, cultural and economic condition.

2) Ways must be found to encourage Asians to share their
   - family values,
   - religious traditions, especially their devotion to the Blessed Mother,
   - sense of celebration.

3) In the church it is incongruous to speak of evangelization and education and, at the same time, to remain ignorant of the people being evangelized and educated. Before ministering to specific Asians, the church should first conduct an in-depth study of their cultures to avoid the repeated mistake of blending and homogenizing the various Asian groups.

4) Asians must be called forth to minister from leadership positions and should be adequately prepared to serve others, mainly from their own people.

5) Many Asians are not accustomed to parish boundaries and consequently seldom formally register within a parish. Therefore, there is a need to directly approach Asians within the home to evangelize. This should be the function of trained lay ministers, preferably Asians themselves.

Diocesan Education Office

1) The Education Office is more effective when it is representative of the people

in the diocese. Therefore, if a significant number of Asian students are enrolled in the Catholic schools,the office should have at least one Asian staff member.

2) The office should publish information regarding the different Asian cultures present in the diocese: percentages, history, demographic characteristics, values, religious devotions, customs, art, music, festivities, family structures, and basic governing principles.

3) The office should engage in regular collaboration and cooperation with local colleges and universities to provide scholarships and low cost programs for the poor.

4) The office should investigate and pursue public and private subsidies to reduce school tuition, thereby increasing educational opportunities.

Catholic Schools

1) Catholic educators are to be prophetic promoters of the mission of Christ by teaching students, from every educational discipline, to interpret the signs of the time in the light of the Gospel and commit their given aptitudes and qualities "to enlarge the human family." (*Populorum Progressio*, #17)

2) An important responsibility of Catholic educators, by virtue of their Christian identity, is to free their students from any oppressing conditions such as inequality of opportunities and discrimination of any kind.

3) Language plays a powerful role in creating emotional responses. The significance given to words in the early stages of learning prepares children for understanding or for prejudice. Educators should make every effort to learn Asian

> "*As a minority parent, I have to face the difference between Chinese and American cultures and values, the potential racial discrimination, the problem of relaxed educational environment, and the difficulties of raising bilingual children. ...My children are not in Catholic schools. That's too expensive.*"
> **A Chinese parent**

phrases and expressions that may serve to build bridges. They should also allow natural communication in the native language during informal activities.

4) High schools which have a number of Asian students should set up "outreach" programs that may allow the students to work with their less privileged brothers and sisters. These programs are geared to develop in the students some social awareness which later may have significant bearing on their ministerial and political options.

5) Cultural celebrations which include the folklore and significant national and religious feast days need to be integrated within the school's special events.

6) Asian cultures need to be studied from an interdisciplinary perspective:
- Cultural values ought to be examined and discussed form different angles during Religion, Social Studies and Literature courses;
- Music, Art, Drama and Physical education may concentrate on the symbolic expression of these values;

- Different food values, clothing and family structures should be compared and analyzed during Home Economics;
- Physical characteristics and their influence on cultural relationships are important topics in Science;
- Mathematics expands the understanding of peoples by the way numbers have been grouped and systematized.

7) The hidden curriculum, which may reflect the norms and values characteristic of Anglo-Saxon culture, must give due consideration to the ethnic groups who may not accept them or value them equally.

8) Teachers need to be educated in countering classroom discrimination by methods such as:
- examining their own attitudes, biases, and stereotypes and trying to identify their origin;
- examining the biases and stereotypes present among the students;
- recognizing biases and stereotyping within textbooks and learning how to deal with them;
- learning to build interdependence among students in order to encourage positive association.

9) If the number of Asian students exceeds 40%, an Asian administrator should be hired to facilitate teacher/student and parent/teacher communication.

Conclusion

It is important for Catholic educators to understand the history, culture and language abilities of their Asian students before planning the curriculum for them. The best approach will be the one that effectively meets the needs of the specific group of Asian students, yet responds to the reality of available resources of personnel and finances.

During the Asian hearings, parents strongly indicated that they wanted their children to learn English in school; however, they were quick to add that they desired their children to learn and use their native language at home. This continued openness to the native language at home can be encouraged by teachers who take time to learn at least a few phrases of the student's language and use it with the child. This acceptance of the native language by the teacher will give a positive message to the child regarding his or her native culture and language.

It is interesting to note that children all over the world learn an additional language in elementary school and begin studying a third language around middle school years. This is not true in the United States.

Kjolseth (1983) states that the United States has spent millions of dollars of public funds teaching foreign languages to English monolinguals while at the same time engaging in systematic efforts to ignore and actively discourage the use and maintenance of these same languages by native speakers.

Kjolseth continues, saying that:

> There is much at stake at home and abroad.... Internationally, our ability to deal effectively with other nations on diplomatic, political, economic, scientific, and social levels is affected by our attitudes towards

other languages and by the availability of appropriately trained persons with bilingual skills. [3]

"This world is multilingual and it is unwise for us to remain on its fringes," Kjolseth cautions.[4]

The Catholic schools of the United States enjoy a reputation of providing quality education. They are now in a position to expand programs that show special sensitivity to the language and cultural backgrounds of Asian students. These programs would respond to students needs in terms of personal and cultural support and language assistance as needed.

Footnotes

1. Jack Kehoe, "Enhancing the Multicultural Climate of the School," *History and Social Science Teacher*, vol. 19, no. 2, December, 1983, p. 65.

2. Theresa McCormick, "Multiculturalism: Some Principles and Issues," *Theory Into Practice*, vol. 23, no. 2, Spring, 1984, p. 94.

3. Rolf Kjolseth, "Cultural Politics of Bilingualism," *Socio-linguistics Today*, May/June, 1983, p. 40.

4. *Ibid.*, p. 48.

CHAPTER IV

Pastoral Structures

As strangers in a different land, each immigrant group has sought to maintain its community. For Catholics, the parish is the basic local unit, and for earlier immigrants the church was the local community in which they could find their identity and continue their traditions. The role of the parish church for current immigrant groups is different from its role in the beginning of the 19th century.

In 1888, Pope Leo XIII brought to the attention of the hierarchy of the United States his concern for the spiritual needs of the immigrants at that time, specifically the Italian immigrants. At the same time, the Catholic Church was struggling to build a Catholic identity in the United States. Vacant land was available to build churches. Today, space in urban areas is unavailable or costly, and the Catholic Church is seen as a well-established entity in American society. In many situations, the people of a parish community are from a plurality of ethnic groups, and the climate of cultural pluralism acknowledges and affirms distinctive ethnic traditions. With the new Code of Canon Law, the community dimension of the parish has become central and the pastoral intent of the law is to promote the stability of that community for the people.

While parishes continue to serve the new immigrants, other ways of making sure that their pastoral needs are being met have also evolved.

The Parish

There are four ways in which the parish provides a support community for various ethnic groups and to new immigrant groups:

1) Through an integrated parish. It is one in which all services of a parish meet the needs of the various groups and where many different groups participate in all of the important structures of a parish. The success of this model depends

upon the complete involvement of all ethnic groups. For example, for an Asian community, it would mean that the parish evangelization program, the parish liturgy, and other parish outreach ministries can only be successful and meaningful to the people when Asian leaders participate in the parish council as well as various parish committees.

Ideally, this can be seen in the reflection of Pope John Paul II on the need of ecclesial integration. He notes:

> In the sphere of migration, any attempt to accelerate or delay integration, or any insertion whatsoever, especially when inspired by an attitude of nationalistic supremacy, whether political or social, can only suffocate or compromise that desirable plurality of voices, which arises from the right to liberty of integration which the migrant faithful have in every particular Church, in which reciprocal acceptance among the groups forming it is born from mutual respect for culture. On the strength of this right to integration the specific ecclesiality, which the migrants bring with them from the churches of origin, does not become a motive of alienation or estrangement from the unity of their own faith, in as much as it is universal, catholic. In this manner the catholicity of the Church becomes evident, in her ethnic and cultural variety: and this catholicity implies a complete openness towards others, a readiness to share and live the same ecclesial communion. (Pope John Paul II's message regarding the observance of World Migrant's Day, 1985)

2) Through a personal parish. On a practical pastoral level, the structure which some Asian Catholic communities can adopt is the personal parish. This is described in Canon 518:

> As a general rule a parish is to be territorial, that is it embraces all the Christian faithful within a certain territory; whenever it is judged useful, however, personal parishes are to be established based upon rite, language, the nationality of the Christian faithful within some territory or even upon some other determining factor.

It is quite clear from this canon that the intent of the church is to ensure that the migrant Christian receives pastoral assistance to guarantee him/her the free exercise of the Christian's rights within the framework of the person's Christian life.

> *"What do the Chinese people want? A lot. They want to feel welcome. However, they feel like they are being an intrusion (intruders in the society in which they are). This is how they feel in the Church which they resent very much. They used to experience the goodness of the Catholic Church at home. That is not how they experience it here. Many have left the Church because they engage in two jobs and want to stay ahead by going to school. Protestants are trying to create a sense of warm welcome.*
>
> **A Chinese sister**

No attempt must be made to apply pressure to assimilate, or integrate into the ordinary. Any such activity would be totally extraneous to the intentions of the church.

Personal parishes are frequently requested and supported by resources of a particular ethnic group. Sometimes the physical facilities for such parishes are located in under-utilized or no longer occupied diocesan buildings.

3) Through a culturally pluralistic parish. This is one physical parish which shares facilities with two or more ethnic ministries. The parish Mass schedule on a weekend is multi-lingual, e.g. the following: on Saturday, 4:00 pm, English; 5:30 pm, Vietnamese; on Sunday, 8:00 am, Laotian; 9:00 am, English; 10:00 am, Spanish; 11:30 am, English; 1:00 pm, Vietnamese. Due to the language differences, many Asian Catholic communities fit into this mode. One serious shortcoming is the fragmentation of the parish community unless serious and regular efforts are made to bring the leaders of all the ethnic communities together and to celebrate the major feasts of the Church together.

4) Through an assimilating parish. In this type of parish you might hear the following: "This is America. Why don't they learn English? Why don't they do the same thing as we do here?" This type of parish does not take into consideration other people's values, customs, cultural norms and gifts. The underlying philosophy of this model is "Americanization" of immigrants. In this type of parish, ethnic groups feel unappreciated and unwanted.

Other Structures

Episcopal Vicars for Ethnic Ministry

In a number of dioceses, episcopal vicars are appointed to be responsible for ethnic apostolates. This may be either for a specific ethnic group or for all ethnic ministries. Examples of these are an Episcopal Vicar for Southeast Asians, an Episcopal Vicar for Koreans, an Episcopal Vicar for Ethnic Ministries. This position is promoted in Canon 476:

As often as the correct governance of the diocese requires it, the diocesan bishop can also appoint one or several episcopal vicars, who possess the same ordinary power which the universal law gives to the vicar general according to the following canons either in a determined section of the diocese or in a certain type of business or over the faithful of a determined rite or over certain groups of persons.

An Overall Ethnic or Pastoral Office

In some dioceses, an office is established as part of the diocesan structure to oversee the ethnic ministries which includes the Asian ministries and/or apostolates, e.g. an Office of Pastoral Services, Secretariat of Ethnic Ministry Services, or an Office of Multicultural Ministry Services.

Individual Ethnic Apostolates

These are diocesan offices which assist in ministry to one particular ethnic group. These offices usually cover the larger ethnic groups in a diocese or are established to serve groups with particular needs such as socio-economic distress, or refugees.

These offices may or may not be located at diocesan headquarters, the later affording the important flexibility of being where the needs are and being in frequent touch with the people. They are usually provided with some budget from the diocese which enables the apostolate to have an office and some support staff.

Ethnic Pastoral Centers

As an alternative to a national or personal parish, some ethnic groups have come together at a pastoral center which provides a focus for social activities, community outreach, ethnic celebrations. Some have provided various social services, for example, to their elderly. These centers do not necessitate the canonical authorization which a parish requires. Other names which are used are centers, clubs or societies. Hence, we might have an Indochinese Catholic Center, a Korean Catholic Center, a Samoan Catholic Club, a Federation of Tongan Catholic Societies.

Chaplains

Another pastoral structure which is canonically prescribed by the Church is the office of a chaplain, as Canon 564 states: "A chaplain is a priest to whom is entrusted in a stable manner the pastoral care, at least in part, of some community or particular group of the Christian faithful, to be exercised in accord with universal and particular law."

This canon has pastoral implications for many of the Asian Catholics in this country because of their recent arrival or rapid change in circumstances. It continues: "To the extent it is possible, chaplains are to be appointed for those who cannot avail themselves of the ordinary care of a pastor because of the condition of their lives, such as migrants, exiles, refugees, nomads, etc."

Liaisons

Because a chaplain must canonically be a priest, and in many situations laypersons are providing for the pastoral care of ethnic groups, a different term has evolved. A layperson may be designated as the "liaison" for a particular ethnic group.

Both chaplains and liaisons are often provided when the group which they serve is scattered throughout a diocese rather than concentrated in a particular area.

All of these structures and variations of parochial situations have evolved as the needs of the various and increasingly numerous cultural groups arrive under differing circumstances. Hence, in one diocese several different structures may be present, with varied groups having different channels of relationship to the local church. The structures for one ethnic group may also vary within one diocese, e.g., Miami may have a personal parish for Haitians and also chaplains for other Haitians. Needs vary, as also do the way in which dioceses are organized. Resources and initiative can be limited; personnel availability, especially when linguistic capability is necessary, may differ. Consequently, it is difficult to impose consistent structures. Rather, an awareness of the strengths and weaknesses of each may ensure the effectiveness of all of these pastoral modes.

CHAPTER V

Holidays, Celebrations and Religious Feasts

CHINESE

New Year:

Chinese New Year falls in late January or early February and marks the beginning of the Lunar New Year. On this day, the Chinese feel they should have a long vacation after a hard year's work. The New Year is their day to give thanks to their ancestors for their existence. Special foods are prepared, presents and goods are exchanged, and hospitality, friendship and most importantly family reunions are common on this day. (The Vietnamese and Koreans also celebrate this occasion.)

Lantern Festival:

On the 15th day after New Year's Day, lanterns of all colors and shapes are displayed in imitation of the first Full Moon in the Lunar calendar month. Many puzzles are written on the lanterns, and whoever solves the puzzles is given a prize. Sweet rice dumplings stuffed with red beans or sesame paste are served. This marks the official ending of the New Year holidays, and the businesses resume the following day.

Ching-Ming (Ancestor's Day):

On March 15th of the Lunar calendar, Chinese families visit their ancestors' graves to plant flowers and clean the site. They bring along a variety of foods and drinks as offerings to be lined-up ceremoniously in front of the tombs; then, they enjoy a picnic for the whole family.

Dragon Boat Festival:

On the 5th day of the fifth month, there is a traditional commemoration of the Poet, Chu-yuan, who drowned himself in protest against the King of Ch'u Kingdom. This loyal poet was unwilling to witness the ruin of his beloved country, as were the people of the Ch'u Kingdom who threw sweet rice, meat and eggs wrapped in leaves (tzung-tze) into the river to feed the hungry fish and, thus, protect the body of the poet. Today, people commemorate the loyalty of Chu-yuan by eating tzung-tze and by throwing it into the river to feed his ghost. In addition, there is a contest of Dragon boats for entertainment.

Mid-Autumn Moon Festival:
On the full moon night of mid-August, considered the brightest of the year, Chinese usually gather outside to appreciate the beauty of the moon and to enjoy the fruit moon cakes—a round paste cake filled with sweet or salted seed powders. According to ancient Chinese mythology, a beautiful woman, Chang-ho, was supposed to share an elixir of immortality with her husband. Out of curiosity, Chang-ho tried to sample the elixir behind her husband's back but was caught. In haste, she swallowed it entirely and floated up to the moon without her husband. Her only companion was a rabbit. People look for the shadow of Chang-ho and the rabbit on this Moon Feast.

The moon cakes are also associated with the expulsion of the Mongols. In the long rule by the Mongols, Chinese plotted revolts by sending messages stuffed in moon cakes.

Double-Nine Day:
The ninth day of the ninth lunar month has been perceived by Chinese as the most comfortable day of the year in terms of weather. Chinese custom sets aside this day for mountain climbing and for outdoor activity.

PHILIPPINE

Simbang Gabi or Misas de Aguinaldo:
Misas de Aguinaldo (the Dawn Mass) originated in Mexico in 1587, when Fray Diego de Soria solicited permission from the Pope to hold the nine day devotional Christmas Masses outdoors because of the large number of people attending. These Masses were held at 4:00 in the morning to accommodate the farmers during harvest season. Today, this spiritual preparation for Christmas continues with residents attending Mass at this hour without question. After the service, traditional foods such as puto-bumbong, a sugary rice served with coconut, and salabat (ginger) tea. The novena ends with Midnight Mass on Christmas Eve, known as Misa de Gallo because of the early hour it is celebrated.

Santo Nino Devotion:
The devotion to Santo Nino goes back to 1521 when Magellan landed on the shores of Cebu to convert the people to Christianity. King Humabon accepted the faith and, after having received a small statuette of the Christ Child, his wife also received Christianity. However, Magellan's death in battle on the island of Mactan, where Christianity was not well received, raised much uncertainty about the new

religion and its power. The people tried to burn all Christian symbols, including the statue of the Child Jesus; but despite all efforts, the statue could not be destroyed. It then disappeared and was not seen for 44 years.

After Magellan's death, Miguel Lopez de Lagaspi lead another fight for Christianity, but this time, the people of Cebu fought back. During this battle a fire broke out and ravaged the town and the people fled to the hills. Afterwards, the little statuette of the Christ Child was found, unharmed and dressed in velvet with a red cap on his head. The statue was presented to Lagaspi, who declared that a church would be dedicated to the Holy Child on the site where the statue was found.

After 44 years, the miraculous return of the Santo Nino restored the people's faith in Christianity. Today, devotions to Santo Nino usually take place on the second or third Sunday of January.

Salubong:

Salubong is a Filipino Easter Celebration at dawn. "Salubong" means "encounter" or "meeting" and in conjunction with Easter, it refers to the meeting of the Risen Christ and his mother at dawn. Based on the intimate mother-son relationship between Mary and Jesus, Filipinos have always assumed the Risen Christ appeared to his mother before anyone else, even though no such meeting is ever mentioned in the scriptures. It is from this belief that the rite of Salubong comes.

> "*The initial stage in ministry to the Hmong must be a welcoming. It is not that we don't know how to do that, but rather we don't want to do it. That is an indictment.*"
> **A priest ministering with the Asian community**

Flores de Mayo:

Flores de Mayo is a very popular tradition expressing love and devotion to Mary. In May, flowers are gathered early in the morning to be offered to the Blessed Mother at an afternoon service. From this comes the term "Flores de Mayo", translated as the May flower devotion to the Blessed Virgin Mother. The main purpose of this celebration is to renew the Marian spirit of the people. The festivity includes the Mass and procession of the statue to the Blessed Virgin. After the Church service, the community gathers for social celebration.

Feast of St. Lorenzo Ruiz and Companions (September 28):

This feast is a celebration of the beatification of the protomartyr of the Philippines, St. Lorenzo Ruiz who was martyred in Nagasaki with 9 companions from Japan, 4 from Spain, 1 from Italy and 1 from France.

INDIAN

Indian Catholics celebrate several feasts and festivals during the year. Besides the feast of Our Lord, they celebrate the feast days of saints in common with other rites in the Church. The celebrations to some extent are colored by the culture of the country. These are some of the important feasts among the three rites of Indian Catholics: the Oriental Rite, the Syro-Malabar Rite and the Malankara Rite.

Christmas (December 25):
Indian Catholics belonging to all three Rites celebrate Christmas along with the Universal Church on December 25th. Midnight Mass, carol singing, Christmas trees, and a solemn procession are the highlights of the day.

Epiphany (January 6):
This feast, though observed everywhere, is solemnly celebrated by some parishes, where the festivities may last three or four days.

St. Sebastian:
Devotion to St. Sebastian is popular in the Syro-Malabar Rite. The feast is celebrated solemnly in almost every parish. Some parishes celebrate this feast as a major festival which may last several days.

St. Joseph (March 19):
This feast is celebrated by every group of Indian Catholics.

The Annunciation (March 25):
This is a very important feast in the Malankara Rite.

St. Peter (June 29):
This feast is solemnly celebrated by the Malankara Rite in India.

St. George (April 23):
Devotion to St. George is popular in the oriental Rite of India. Many parishes celebrate this feast as a major feast lasting for several days.

Good Friday/Easter:
The season of Lent with its culmination in Good Friday and Easter is one of the most beautiful Christian experiences in India. On Good Friday everyone goes to church and participates in the services. Solemn Way of the Cross processions through the public streets, and huge processions carrying the statue of the crucified Christ are very common. Easter is celebrated with much festivity.

St. Thomas (July 3):
St. Thomas Christians observe the memory of St. Thomas' death on July 3rd. Liturgical celebrations and processions are some highlights of the day. St. Thomas Christians celebrate this as their Community Day. In many places, public meetings

and cultural programs help teach children about their traditions.

All Saints and All Souls Days (November 1 & 2):
Everyone tries to observe these days. On All Souls Day, a prayerful procession to the cemetery is common.

Monthly Devotions:
March (St. Joseph), May (Our Blessed Virgin Mary), June (Sacred Heart), November (Souls in purgatory): During these months, in the churches as well as at homes, meditations and special prayers are performed. Children decorate the family altars with flowers, and candles are burned.

Special Devotions:
Eight days of abstinence, September 1-8, are observed in honor of the Blessed Virgin Mary's birth. Many people observe these days by attending religious services in the church, fasting, and eating only vegetarian food.
Novenas: Perpetual Novenas in honor of Our Lady, St. Joseph and St. Jude are held in several churches in India.

Special Celebrations in Malankara Rite:
The Malankara Rite observes **September 20th as Reunion Day**, which celebrates the beginning of the Malankara Rite.
Mar Ivanios Day (July 15) is solemnly celebrated in the Malankara Rite. Mar Ivanios was the first bishop of the Malankara Rite, and was instrumental in the origin of the Rite. This day celebrates the reunion of the venerable bishop and his companions to the Catholic Church.

JAPANESE

New Year's Day—*Oshogatsu* (January 1):
While January 1 is the official national holiday, the first three days of January are celebrated as the "New Year."

Adults' Day—*Seijin no Hi* (January 15):
On this national holiday, young men and women who are twenty celebrate their coming of age.

Paul Miki and Companions, Martyrs (February 6):
The Japanese Catholics remember Paul Miki and his companions who were canonized in 1862. These protomartyrs included 20 Japanese, 5 Spaniards and 1 Mexican.

***Hinamatsuri* (March 3):**
This is a traditional celebration for girls. In homes, dolls are displayed, especially a complete set representing the Emperor and Empress and their court.

Equinox Days—*Ohigan* (March 21 and September 23):
These days, one in spring, and one in autumn, are national holidays when Japanese honor the dead, especially their parents or grandparents. Visits are made to Buddhist temples and cemeteries.

Constitution Day—*Kinpo Kinenbi* (May 3):
This national holiday commemorates the inauguration of Japan's Constitution.

Boys' Festival—*Tango no Sekku* (May 5):
This is a traditional celebration for boys. Great carp streamers fly over rooftops of homes with sons. Warrior dolls and samurai arms are displayed in homes.

Obon (August 13-15):
The souls of ancestors are honored during this very important traditional celebration. Japanese return to their homes, often in rural areas; special foods are prepared for the return of the ancestor's soul.

Respect for the Aged Days—*Keiro no Hi* (September 15):
All businesses and government offices are closed on this national holiday.

Culture Day—*Bunka no Hi* (November 3):
Originally celebrated as the Emperor Meiji's birthday, this national holiday now promotes respect for Japan's cultural heritage.

Seven (7), Five (5), Three (3)—*Shichi-Go-San* (November 15):
Children who are 7, 5 and 3 years old, go to visit shrines and dress in ceremonial attire.

Labor-Thanksgiving Day—*Kinro Kansha no Hi* (November 23):
This is a national holiday to give thanks for the harvest of rice.

The Emperor's Birthday—*Tenno Tanjobi* (December 23):
On this national holiday, the public is invited to enter the Imperial Palace to pay their respects to the Emperor on his birthday.

KOREAN

Chusok (Harvest Moon Festival):
Celebrated on August 15 of the Lunar calendar, this feast is similar to our American Thanksgiving. Activities on this day are family-oriented. An abundance of food is prepared and generations of families gather to celebrate and to thank God for all blessings. A visit to the cemetery to remember the deceased members of the family is also an important ritual on this day.

Feast of 103 Martyr Saints of Korea:

In 1865, the number of Koreans converting to Catholicism swelled to such great numbers that it provoked severe persecutions from the Confucian government. As a result, thousands of converts died, 93 of whom were canonized saints by Pope John Paul II in Korea in 1984. Ten French missionaries were also canonized at the same time. The heroic virtues of these 103 martyrs are observed by the Church on September 20, and by Korean Catholics the following Sunday.

Korean New Year:

Like the Chinese, the Koreans celebrate their New Year by the Lunar calendar. It is for them, too, a day to honor their ancestors. It is celebrated with family rituals, special food and traditional games. Korean Catholics celebrate Mass in remembrance of their deceased ancestors and relatives.

VIETNAMESE

Lunar New Year (Tet):

This traditional holiday is determined by the Lunar calendar and usually occurs during the month of February. It is the biggest event of the year in Vietnam and is usually celebrated for three days. It is a combination of family reunion, Spring festival and a national holiday. "Tet" is also considered everyone's birthday since individual birthday celebrations do not exist and because everyone is one year older on "Tet." Again "Tet" is a time to remember ancestors, visit family and friends, correct all faults and celebrate.

> "*There is a growing abuse among children and teenagers. Young girls do not feel appreciated for who they are. They have no where to turn. They can't turn to American adults for American adults don't understand their culture. They can't turn to their Asian parents for their parents would ask from them absolute obedience.*"
>
> **A sister ministering with the Asian community**

Mid-Autumn Festival (Trung Thu):

This holiday is celebrated by Vietnamese of all walks of life. It falls on the 15th day of the 8th month of the lunar calendar. According to popular belief and legends, the moon is the dwelling place of a beautiful fairy named Hang Nga. On this occasion, grown-ups enjoy the beauty of the full moon while eating moon-shaped cakes and drinking tea. This feast is special for children for they enjoy the lion dances and paper lanterns. The moon is a favorite theme of Vietnamese literature.

Vietnamese All Souls Day (Vu-Lan):

This day, dedicated to the virtue of filial piety, falls on the 15th day of the 7th month of the lunar calendar. Vietnamese people offer prayers for the redemption of the sins committed by deceased parents and wandering souls.

Feast of 117 Martyr Saints of Vietnam:

On June 19, 1988, Pope John Paul II canonized the 117 holy martyrs of Vietnam. The Vietnamese Catholics see the Holy Martyrs as having attained the perfect harmony between the Catholic faith and the Vietnamese vital spirit. The Vietnamese vital spirit can only be identified in the traditions and customs of the Vietnamese people. The memorial feast for these holy martyrs is celebrated on November 24 of each year.

CAMBODIAN

New Year:

The biggest religious holiday for the Cambodian people is the New Year and usually begins around April 13th. New Year activities include religious ceremonies, visiting friends and relatives, taking food to the temple and attending classical dance performances.

All Souls Day (Prachum Ben):

This festival usually falls in September and is a day in which prayers are offered up to the souls of those who have died. Every day for two weeks, the people go to the temple to offer a morning meal and return in the evening to hear the monks preach. Balls of rice are offered to the spirits of the dead and on the last day, people visit the temple where the ashes of their ancestors are kept.

Phisak Bauchia:

Another important holiday usually celebrated in May is Phisak Bauchia which commemorates Buddha's birth, enlightenment and death.

Chaul Vuhsa:

This holiday takes place at the beginning of the rainy season and marks the retreat of the "sangha," (Buddhist monks). It is preceded by the ordination of monks and novices. Ordination ceremonies are colorful and elaborate. Accompanied by chanting monks, musicians, relatives and friends, the young men who are to enter the "sangha" are led in procession around the ordination hall. The ceremony is concluded by the abbot's acceptance of the candidates. Soon after the acceptance, the candidates change into the colored garments of the order.

Chenh Vuhsa:

Usually occurring in October, this festival is marked by the monks coming out of retreat. At this time each temple celebrates the "Kathen" festival in which objects such as clothing are given to the "sangha."

Miakh Bauchia:

Miakh Bauchia is usually celebrated during February and marks the Buddha's last sermon.

HMONG

New Year:

The Hmong New Year is the most important celebration, which usually begins in December. Offerings are made to the spirits and ancestors to insure good fortune for the coming year.

LAOTIAN

Lao New Year (Pi Mai):

The Lao New Year—Pi Mai—is the most widespread and popular occasion celebrated by the Lao. It usually occurs between April 13 and 15. Pi Mai stems from an ancient Lao legend in which the daughters of a God offer him thanks for abundant rainfall and the fertility of the earth.

The Lao New Year is a time of rejuvenation and rejoicing. The Lao people give thanks and ask forgiveness for past wrongs. Statuettes of Buddha are cleansed by pouring perfumed water over them, symbolizing purification. The people pray for the well-being of themselves and their loved ones. They then pour water over one another and wish each other a happy New Year. The New Year is also a time for young people to honor their elders with a "Baci" or "wishing well" ceremony, in which the young ones ask for forgiveness of past wrongs they may have committed. The elders then forgive them and wish them a happy New Year.

> "*D*o not say welcome and our door is open, but rather be educated about the newcomers. An outreach program has to be embedded in the parish. The attitude of the clergy which needs to be changed is: 'What I do for you is over and above what my responsibility is.'"
>
> **A Chinese diocesan minister**

Sou Khouan

As mentioned above, the New Year's Baci ceremony is a show of respect to the elders. Another form of this ceremony is known as Sou Khouan and is used to treat "depressed persons."

The Lao people believe that in each person, there are 32 spirits present which give health, happiness and prosperity. A lack of any of these spirits is believed to cause depression, illness and disease. The purpose of "Sou Khouan" is to promote recovery by calling back the spirits that have left a person's body. Misfortune, fear of the unknown, personal defamation and loss of identity, violation of an ancestral tradition, and insulting of one's divinity are all believed to be causes for a person's loss of spirits.

CHAPTER VI

Resources

I. BIBLIOGRAPHY

A Catholic Response to the Asian Presence in the United States, A Report on Asian Hearings conducted by NCEA, USCC Office of Migration and Refugee Services, Pastoral Care of Migrants and Refugees, and New York Archdiocesan Office of Pastoral Research and Planning, 1990.

Amerasia Journal, The national interdisciplinary journal of scholarship, criticism, and literature on Asian and Pacific Americans. Published by the Asian American Studies Center, University of California, Los Angeles, since 1971. *Amerasia* is published twice-yearly, in the spring and fall.

Andres, Thomas D. *Understanding Filipino Values*, New Day Publishers, Quezon City, Philippines, 1981.

Anh, To Thi. *Eastern and Western Cultural Values, Conflict or Harmony?*, East Asian Pastoral Institute, Manila, Philippines, 1975.

Apostolate Profile of the Catholic Communities of the Cambodian, Hmong, Kmhmu, and Laotian People, Office for the Pastoral Care of Migrants and Refugees, Migration and Refugee Services, United States Catholic Conference, Washington, DC, August, 1989.

Archer, Robert. *Vietnam: the Habit of War*, Catholic Institute for International Relations, London, 1983.

Beaver, R. Pierce, et al, ed. *Eerdmans' Handbook to the World's Religions*, Lion Publishing, England, 1982.

Bolts, T. William, SM. *The Catholic Experience in America*, Benzinger, Encino, 1980.

Breunig, Jerome, SJ. *Have You Had Your Rice Today?*, Loyola University Press, Chicago, 1964.

Castillo, Noemi M. *Introduction to Filipino Ministry*, Archdiocese of San Francisco in cooperation with the Office of Pastoral Care of Migrants and Refugees, United States Catholic Conference, San Francisco, CA, 1985.

Castillo, Noemi, ed. *Pastoral Plan for Filipino Ministry*, Office of Filipino Catholic Affairs, San Francisco, CA, 1989.

Chang-mun Kim, Fr. Joseph and John Jae-sun Chung. *Catholic Korea—Yesterday and Today*, Catholic Korea Publishing Company, Korea, 1964.

Charbonnier, Jean. *Guide To The Catholic Church in China*, Catholic Communication, Singapore, 1989.

Ch'him, Sun-Him, Khamchong Luangpraseut and Huynh Dinh Te, *Introduction to Cambodian Culture, Laos Culturally Speaking, Introduction to Vietnamese Culture*, Multifunctional Resource Center, San Diego University, CA, 1989.

Chupungco, Anscar, J. OSB, ed. *Liturgical Renewal in the Philippines*, Maryhill School of Theology, Quezon City, Philippines, 1981.

Clark, Francis X., SJ. *Mission and the Philippines—the Past, Present and Future*, Loyola School of Theology, Ateneo de Manila University Press, Quezon City, Philippines, 1981.

Clark, Allen D. *A History of the Church in Korea*, The Christian Literature Society of Korea, Korea, 1971.

Covell, Dr. John Carter. *Korea's Cultural Roots*, Sixth edition, Hollum International Corp., Elizabeth, NJ, 1983.

De la Torre, Visitacion R. *Patterns of Philippine Life*, Regal Printing Press, Manila, Philippines, 1978.

De Mesa, Jose M. *And God Said "Bahala Na"*, New Day Publishers, Quezon City, Philippines, 1971.

De Mesa, Jose M. *And God Said: "Bahala Na"*, Maryhill Studies 2, Maryhill School of Theology, Quezon City, Philippines, 1981.

Digan, Parig. *Churches in Contestation, Asian Christian Social Protest*, Orbis Books, Maryknoll, New York, 1984.

Duldulao, Manuel, ed. *The Filipinos*, Orea Books, The Philippines, 1987.

Ellis, Msgr. John Tracy. *American Catholicism*, Revised Second edition, The University of Chicago Press, Chicago and London, 1969.

Elwood, Douglas J. and Patricia L. Magdamo, *Christ in the Philippine Context*, New Day Publishers, Quezon City, Philippines, 1971.

Episcopal Commission on Education and Religious Instruction. *Maturing in Christian Faith (National Catechetical Directory of the Philippines)*, Third Revised edition, St. Paul Publication, 1983, 1986.

Fairbanks, John K., Edwin O. Reischauer and Albert M. Craig. *East Asia, Tradition and Transformation*, Revised ed., Boston, Houghton Mifflin Co., 1989.

Fitzpatrick, Joseph P., SJ. *One Church, Many Cultures*, Sheed and Ward, Kansas City, MO, 1987.

Fuerst, Rev. Adrian, OSB, ed. *A Commentary on Seminary Priesthood Enrollment Statistics for 1989 —Part I & II*, vols. 16, 17, no. 1-4, Center for Applied Research in the Apostolate (CARA), Washington, DC, 1989.

Gannon, Thomas M., SJ. *World Catholicism in Transition*, New York, Macmillan, 1988.

Gardner, Robert W., Bryant Robey and Peter C. Smith. "Asian American: Growth, Change, and Diversity." *Population Bulletin*, vol 40. no. 4, Population Reference Bureau, Inc., October, 1985.

Gatbonton, Esperanza. *A Heritage of Saints*, Editorial Associates Ltd., Manila and Hong Kong, 1979.

Gremillion, Joseph. ed. *The Church and Culture*, University of Notre Dame Press, Notre Dame, IN, 1985.

Guthrie, George M. ed. *Six Perspectives on the Philippines*, MDB Printing, Makati, Philippines, 1968.

Ha, Kim Chi. *The Gold Crowned Jesus and Other Writings*, Orbis Books, Maryknoll, New York, 1978.

Hardy, Richard P. ed. *The Philippine Bishops Speak (1968-1983)*, Maryhill School of Theology, Quezon City, Philippines, 1984.

Indochincese Refugee Education Guides, National Indochinese Clearinghouse, Center for Applied Linguistics, Arlington, VA.

Kalton, Michael C. "Korean Ideas and Values," *Inculturation*, Winter, 1987.

Lawyers Committee for Human Rights. *Kampuchea: After the Worst*, A Report on Current Violations of Human Rights, Washington, DC, August, 1985.

Kim, Edward H. *Facts About Korea*, 18th Revised edition, Holly Corporation Publishers, Seoul, Korea, 1985.

Kung, Hans and Julia Ching. *Christianity and Chinese Religions*, Doubleday, New York, 1989.

Ladany, Lazlo. *The Catholic Church in China*, Freedom House, New York, 1987.

Lazzarotto, Angelo. *The Catholic Church in China in Post-Mao China*, Holy Spirit Study Centre, Hong Kong, 1982.

Lynch, Frank, SJ. et al. *The Filipino Family, Community and Nation*, Ateneo de Manila University Press, Quezon City, Philippines, 1978.

Lynch, Frank, SJ. "Folk Catholicism in the Philippines," *Society, Culture and the Filipino*, HRAF Area Handbook on the Philippines, 1956.

MacInnis, Donald. *Religion in China Today, Policy and Practice*, Maryknoll, Orbis Books, New York, 1989.

McGuire, Anthony E. ed. *Light of Nations*, Archdiocese of San Francisco, CA, 1985.

Mendez, Pax and Landa F. Jocano. *The Filipino Family and Its Rural and Urban Orientation*, Centro Escolar University Research and Development Center, Manila, Philippines, 1979.

Mercado, Leonardo N., SVD. *Elements of Filipino Theology*, Divine Word University Publications, Tacloban City, Philippines, 1975.

Mercado, Leonard N., SVD. *Elements of Filipino Philosophy*, Revised edition, Divine Word University Publications, Tacloban City, Philippines, 1976.

Mercado, Leonard N., SVD. *Filipino Religious Psychology*, Divine Word University Publications, Tacloban City, Philippines, 1977.

Mercado, Leonard N., SVD. *Christ in the Philippines*, Divine Word University Publications, Tacloban City, Philippines, 1982.

Mercado, Leonard N., SVD. *Elements of Filipino Ethics*, Divine Word University Publications, Tacloban City, Philippines, 1982.

Mortell, Rev. Anthony, SSC. "Korean Catholic Community in the United States, Present Status & Future Prospects," Third Annual Conference of Korean American University Professors Association, Los Angeles, CA, November 3-5, 1989.

Nudas, Alfeo G., SJ. *God With Us: The 1986 Philippine Revolution*, Loyola School of Theology, Manila, Philippines, 1979.

On Korean Laborers—A Perspective Paper and Data Base, Maryknoll, New York, April, 1988.

Panopi, Isabel, et al. *General Sociology: Focus on the Philippines*, Asian Social Institute, Manila, Philippines, 1981.

Park, Rev. Augustine. *A Report on the Pastoral Care of Korean Immigrants*, Presented to the National Conference of Catholic Bishops, Office of Pastoral Care of Migrants and Refugees, 1985.

Pastoral Care of Vietnamese Catholics in the United States, A Preliminary Report, Pastoral Care of Migrants and Refugees, Bishops' Committee on Migration and Tourism, National Conference of Catholic Bishops, Washington, DC, September, 1985.

Pastoral Plan for Mission to Southeast Asian People in the Archdiocese of Boston, Archdiocese of Boston, MA, 1989.

People on the Move: A Compendium of Church Documents on the Pastoral Concern for Migrants and Refugees, Bishops' Committee on Priestly Formation, Bishops' Committee on Migration, National Conference of Catholic Bishops, Washington, DC, June, 1988.

Proceedings of the First Meeting of the Cambodian, Hmong and Laotian Apostolate in the Catholic Church in the United States, Office for the Pastoral Care of Migrants and Refugees, Bishops' Committee on Migration and Tourism, National Conference of Catholic Bishops, Washington, DC, 1985.

Proceedings of the Fourth Annual Meeting of the Cambodian, Hmong, Kmhmu and Laotian Apostolates, "Lay People and Migration," Office for the Pastoral Care of Migrants and Refugees, Bishops' Committee on Migration, National Conference of Catholic Bishops, Washington, DC, 1988.

Profiles of the Highland Lao Communities in the United States, Final Report, U.S. Department of Health and Human Services, Office of Refugee Resettlement, November, 1988.

Ramirez, Mina M. *A Phenomenology of Philippine Socio-Cultural Reality*, Asian Social Institute, Manila, Philippines, 1981.

Ramirez, Mina M. *Understanding Philippine Social Realities through the Filipino Family*, Asian Social Communication Center, Manila, Philippines, 1984.

Reasons for Living and Hoping: Proceedings from the Multi-Disciplinary, Inter-Religious Conference on the Spiritual and Psycho-Social Needs of Southeast Asian Refugee

Children and Youth Resettled in the United States, The International Catholic Child Bureau, Inc. (ICCB), New York, 1989.

Refugee Reports, A News Service of the U.S. Committee for Refugees, vol. IX, no. 12, December 16, 1988.

Refugees from Cambodia, A Look at History, Culture and the Refugee Crisis, Refugee Information Series, Migration and Refugee Services, United States Catholic Conference, Washington, DC, March, 1984.

Refugees from Laos, A Look at History, Culture and the Refugee Crisis, Refugee Information Series, Migration and Refugee Services, United States Catholic Conference, Washington, DC, March, 1984.

Roces, Alfredo, R., ed. *Filipino Heritage: The Making of a Nation*, vol. 1-10, Vera Reyes, Inc. Philippines.

Schumacher, John N., SJ. *Readings in Philippine Church History*, Loyola School of Theology, Manila, Philippines, 1979.

Southeast Asian Refugee Studies, Newsletter, A publication of the Southeast Asian Refugee Studies Project, Center for Urban and Regional Affairs, University of Minnesota. Glenn L. Hendricks, coordinator; Bruce Downing, editor-in-chief. Published quarterly in January, April, July, and October.

Takaki, Ronald. *Strangers from a Different Shore, A History of Asian Americans*, Little, Brown and Company, Boston, 1989.

The Catholic Church in Korea, Bicentennial Episcopal Commission Seoul, Korea, January, 1984.

The Family in Migration: A Report on the Cambodian, Hmong, Kmhmu and Laotian Apostolate, Pastoral Care of Migrants and Refugees, Bishops' Committee on Migration, National Conference of Catholic Bishops, Washington, DC, 1987.

The People and Cultures of Cambodia, Laos, and Vietnam, Center for Applied Linguistics, Washington, DC, 1981.

Thernstrom, Stephan, ed. *Harvard Encyclopedia of American Ethnic Groups*, Harvard University Press, Cambridge, MA, 1980.

Together a New People: Pastoral Statement on Migrants and Refugees, National Conference of Catholic Bishops. Washington, DC, November, 1986.

Tomasi, Rev. Silvano M., CS. "The Asian Presence: Richness in Diversity," *Catholic Evangelization*, January/February, 1989.

We, the Asian and Pacific Islander Americans, U.S. Department of Commerce, Bureau of the Census. U.S. Government Printing Office, Washington, DC, 1980.

Welcome into the Community of Faith, A Report on the Cambodian, Hmong, and Laotian Apostolate, Pastoral Care of Migrants and Refugees, National Conference of Catholic Bishops, Washington, DC, 1986.

Whyte, Bob. *Unfinished Encounter, China and Christianity*, Collins, Glasgow, Great Britain, 1988.

Wurth, Elmer, ed. *Papal Documents Related to the New China, 1937-1984*, Maryknoll, Orbis Books, New York, 1985.

II. RESOURCE CENTERS

Bishop Salas Cambodian
Catholic Center
7308 Pine Drive
Annandale, Virginia 22003
(703) 642-5478

Cambodian Ministry
c/o St. Patrick Rectory
282 Suffolk Street
Lowell, Massachusetts 01854
(508) 459-0561

East Coast Hmong Ministry
239 Oxford Street
Providence, Rhode Island 02905
(401) 781-7210

Filipino Catholic Affairs
Archdiocese of San Francisco
445 Church Street
San Francisco, California 94114
(415) 565-3682

Hmong Apostolate
c/o St. John Cathedral
2814 Mariposa Street
Fresno, California 93721
(209) 485-6210

Hmong Catholic Center
951 E. 5th Street
St. Paul, Minnesota 55106
(612) 771-4644

Indian Catholic Mission
c/o St. Bernard Church
7341 Cottage Street
Philadelphia, Pennsylvania 19136
(215) 333-0446

Indian Ministry
c/o Rev. A. Moses Kallarackal, CMI
Holy Family Church
21 Nassau Avenue
Brooklyn, New York 11222

Laotian Pastoral Center
3508 Maurice Avenue
Fort Worth, Texas 76111
(817) 831-2336

National Association of Asian and
Pacific American Education
(NAAPAE)
c/o 310 Eight Street, Suite 220
Oakland, California 94607
(415) 834-9455

National Association for the Education and Advancement of Cambodian, Laotian and Vietnamese Americans (NAFAE)
c/o Khamchong Luangpraseut
Indochinese Program
1405 French Street
Santa Ana, California 92701
(714) 558-5729

National Pastoral Center for the
Chinese Apostolate
105 Mosco Street, 2nd floor
New York, New York 10013
(212) 732-8558

National Pastoral Center for the
Korean Apostolate
c/o St. Andrew Kim Church
257 Central Avenue
Orange, New Jersey 07050
(201) 672-6650

National Pastoral Center for the
Vietnamese Apostolate
c/o Mary Queen of Vietnam Church
P.O. Box 29745
New Orleans, Louisiana 70189
(504) 254-5660

III. CATECHETICAL MATERIALS

CHINESE

Hymnals:
Huang Le Nien Hwa—Happy Songs, published by SVD, Chiayi City, Taiwan, 1979.
Sung Yang— Hong Kong Catholic Hymnal, Hong Kong Truth Society, 1976.
Sheng Ke Xuang Ji—Selection of Hymns, Vincentian Fathers, Kaohsiung, 1987.
Sheng Yung—Selection of Psalms (Prima Missa), Hong Kong, 1956.
San Sung—Selection of Catholic Songs, Hong Kong, 1982.

Catechetical Materials:
   Catechism of Catholic Doctrine, New Catechism published by the Synodal Commission with English translation, Catholic Truth Society, Hong Kong, October, 1985.
   Catholic Faith, (Chinese only) New Catechism published by the Synodal Commission, Wisdom Publisher, Taipei City, Taiwan, ROC, June, 1970.
   A Collection of Catholic Catechism, (Chinese only), New Catechism, edited by Rev. John B. Liu and Rev. Joseph Yi, Hua Ming Press, Taipei City, Taiwan, ROC, August, 1983.
   The Most Beautiful Story—Bible, (Chinese only), New Catechism, edited by the Daughters of St. Paul, St. Paul Catholic Center, Taipei, Taiwan, ROC, December, 1986.
   Questions and Answers About the Catholic Faith, Taiwan, ROC.
   Correspondence Course in Catechesis, Rev. Joseph Chao, Archdiocese of New York, NY.

Resources for Catechetical Materials:

Neighborhood Bible Studies
Box 222
Dobbs Ferry, New York 10522
(Chinese and Japanese editions)

The Daughters of St. Paul
76, Ha Keng Hau Village
Shatin, N.T.
Hong Kong

The Daughters of St. Paul
66 San Tai Road
Hsinchuang
Taipei, Taiwan 24232
R.O.C.

INDIAN

Resources for Catechetical Materials:

Carmen Bookstore
Cotton Hill
Trivanbrum 695014
Kerala, India

The Daughters of St. Paul
143, Waterfield Road—Bandra
Bombay 400050
India

Janatha Book
Thodupuzha 685584
Kerala, India

Rev. David Pattath
Gallilea Chiyyaram Institute
Trichur 680026
Kerala, India

St. Paul Book Center
Broadway
Ernakulam, Cochin 682011
Kerala, India

JAPANESE

The catechetical materials listed below are available in Japanese at the following publishers/book stores:

Chuo Shuppansha
Yotsuya 1-2, Shinjuku-ku
Tokyo, 160
Japan

Akashi Shobo
Narita Nishi 3-9-22
Suginami-ku
Tokyo, 166
Japan

Joshi Paurokai (The Daughters of
St. Paul)
Akasaka 8-12-42
Minato-Ku
Tokyo, 107
Japan

Kyoto Catechetical Center
Niomondori Shintakakura Higashi Iru
Kita Monzencho 469
Sakyoku, Kyoto 606
Japan
(Inquiries may be made in English or
Japanese.)

Oriens
28-5, Matsubara 2 Chome
Setagaya-ku
Tokyo 156
Japan

Books for Children Grades 1-6:

Iesusu-sama to issho (Together with Jesus), Chuo Shuppansha, publisher.
Kami-sama kiite: Kodomo to Misa (Lower Grades: Children and Mass), Joshi Paurokai, publisher.
Boku to watasi no hasseitai (My First Communion), Oriens, publisher.
Nakama ni natta Misa (My Mass), Oriens, publisher.
Kodomo no Seisho (Kyuyaku) (Child's Bible: Old Testament), Chuo Shuppansha,

publisher.

Kodomo no Seisho (Shinyaku) (Child's Bible: New Testament), Chuo Shuppansha, publisher.

Seisho Monogatari Kyu-shin (Two volumes: Old and New Testament in easy language with drawings for middle to upper grades), Joshi Paurokai, publisher.

Shogakusei no Katekejisu (Catechesis for Grade School children), Oriens, publisher.

Books for Junior High School Students:

Anatatachi wo tomo to yobu (Catechetical course for JHS), Joshi Paurokai, publisher.

Kirisuto no kyokai no rekishi (History of Christ's Church), Oriens, publisher.

Katorikku no Shinko (The Catholic Faith), Akashi Shobo, publisher.

Kami to tomo ni Aruku (Walking with God), Chuo Shuppansha, publisher.

Books for Senior High School Students and Adults:

Ai to Yurushi to Inori to (Love, Forgiveness & Prayer: Introduction to Christianity for Young Adults), Chuo Shuppansha, publisher.

Nihon 26 Seijinkyosha (The 26 Japanese Martyrs), Chuo Shuppansha, publisher.

Mazaa Teresa to sono Sekai (The World of Mother Teresa), Joshi Paurokai, publisher.

Tomo no Inori (Prayer Book), Joshi Paurokai, publisher.

Books for Adults:

Atarashii Kirisutokyou Nyumon (New Introduction to Christianity), Chuo Shuppansha, publisher.

Katorikku Nyumon (Introduction to Catholicism: Catechism), Chuo Shuppansha, publisher.

Kirisuto no Nanazashi (A Glimpse of Jesus: Looking at Jesus through the Scriptures), Chuo Shuppansha, publisher.

Ai ni ikiru Mazaa Teresa (Mother Teresa), Chuo Shuppansha, publisher.

Kirisuto wo Shiru Tame ni (To Know Jesus: Introduction to Christianity, Vol. 1), Chuo Shuppansha, publisher.

Kirisuto to sono Kyokai (Christ and His Church: Introduction to Christianity, Vol. 2), Chuo Shappansha, publisher.

Kenshin no Hiseki to Seirei (Confirmation and the Holy Spirit), Chuo Shuppansha, publisher.

Seijintachi no Shogai (Lives of the Saints), Chuo Shuppansha, publisher.

Kirisutokyo no Genten toshita no Fukuin (The Gospel as the core of Christianity), Joshi Paurokai, publisher.

Shinyaku Seisho no Iezusu-zo (The Image of Jesus in the New Testament), Joshi Paurokai, publisher.

Inori (How to enter into Deep Prayer by a well-known Carmelite Father), Joshi Paurokai, publisher.

Shu to tomo ni (Jujika no Michiyuki) (Meditative Stations of the Cross), Joshi Paurokai, publisher.

Misa wo Ikiru (Living the Mass: History and Commentary on the Mass), Joshi Paurokai, publisher.

Kirisutokyo to wa Nani ka (Easy Introduction to Christianity), Joshi Paurokai, publisher.

Shinto no Reisei (Spirituality for the Laity), Joshi Paurokai, publisher.

Videos from Joshi Paurokai (Available at Joshi Paurokai and the Kyoto Catechetical Center—see address above.)

Kurisumasu (Christmas), 15 minutes, color.

Mazaa Teresa (Mother Teresa), 20 minutes, color.

Kurisutofaa (Christopher), 25 minutes, color.

Osama no Hoshi (The Kings' Star: story based on the Three Kings), 23 minutes, color.

Iesusama (The Story of Jesus), 20 minutes, color.

Mazaa Teresa to sono Sekai (Documentary on Mother Teresa), 55 minutes, color.

KOREAN

The following catechetical materials are available at:
Mee-Joo Catholic Books
P.O. Box 598
Orange, New Jersey 07051
(201) 672-6274

Catechisms: (Korean only)

Catholic Catechisms, C.C. K.

You Are Invited, Archdiocese of Seoul, South Korea.

The Way to Faith, Rev. Lyu, Bong Ku.

Teachings of Christ, Rev. Oh, Kyoung Whan.

What Are We to Do?, Rev. Park, Do Shick.

Confirmation Catechisms, Archdiocese of Seoul, South Korea.

Bibles:

Old and New Testament.

New Testament. (Large letter)

New Testament. (Medium Letter)

New Testament. (Pocket size)

The New Testament. (English and Korean)

English and Korean Sunday Missal.

Resources for Catechetical Materials:

The Daughters of St. Paul
103 Mi A Dong Do bong Ku
Seoul 132-104
Korea

Catholic Catechetical Institute
54, 1-ga, Changch'ung-dong, Chung-gu
Seoul, 100-391
Korea

Catholic Publishing House
149-2, Changrim-dong, Chung-gu
Seoul, 100-360
Korea

Benedict Press
56-12, 1-ga, Changch'ung-dong,
Chung-gu
Seoul, 100-391
Korea

Bible and Life Publishing Company
116-2, Ch'ongdam-dong, Kangnam-gu
Seoul, 135-100
Korea

PHILIPPINE

Video Cassette Materials:

The Philippines and Its People. Catholic Communications Center, Attn.: Journey of Faith, 441 Church St., San Francisco, CA 94114

The Church in the Philippines. Catholic Communications Center, Attn.: Journey of Faith, 441 Church Street, San Francisco, CA 94114.

Filipino Spirituality. Catholic Communications Center, Attn.: Journey of Faith, 441 Church Street, San Francisco, CA 94114.

Filipinos: Gift to the Church. Catholic Communications Center, Attn.: Journey of Faith, 441 Church Street, San Francisco, CA 94114.

VIETNAMESE

The following catechetical materials can be ordered/purchased from:
Co So Truyen Thong Dan Chua
P. O. Box 1419
Gretna, LA 70053
(504) 392-1630

Prayer Books:

Book of Prayers.
One Hour Adoration of the Blessed Sacrament.
Devotion to the Sacred Hearts of Jesus and Mary.
Devotion to the Blessed Mary.
Family Devotion to the Blessed Virgin Mary.
Sincere Devotion to Madonna.
The Miracle of Our Lady at Binh Trieu.
Meditation of the Passions of our Lord Jesus Christ.

Pastoral Care of the Sick.
Lives of the Saints.
Novena of Our Lady of Perpetual Help.
Life of Jesus Christ.
Saint Martin.
The Second Vatican Council (Vol I).
The Second Vatican Council (Vol. II).
Vietnamese Catholic Family Record Book.

Catechisms:
Basic Catechism.
Christ, the Way to the Father. (ages 8-12)
First Communion—Lessons. (Bilingual)
First Communion—Exercises. (Bilingual)
Children's Catechism.
Catechism for Confirmation—Lessons and Exercises.
Sacramental Catechism.
Entering into the Old Testament.
Entering into the New Testament.
Marriage Catechism: The Way to Love.

Social & Cultural Books:
The Root of the Vietnamese Culture.
The United States and the Global Strategy.
Preparation for the U.S. Naturalization Exam.

Resources for Catechetical Materials:
Congregation of the Co-Redemptrix
P. O. Box 836
Carthage, MO 64836-9990
(417) 358-8296

CAMBODIAN

The following catechetical materials can be ordered/purchased from:
Rev. Rogatien Rondineau, MEP
c/o Bishop Salas Cambodian Catholic Center
7308 Pine Drive
Annandale, VA 22003
(703) 642-5478

Books:
Approaches of Khmer Mentality. (English)
Catechism for Inquirers. (English/Khmer)
Guidelines to Help the Catechumens. (Bilingual)
New Testament. (Khmer)

Psalms. (Bilingual)
Worship.

The bilingual missals (8 volumes) are currently out of print exept the volume for the Ordinary time of the year (Year C), from the Feast of the Holy Trinity to the end of the liturgical year.

New Books:
Accompanying Cambodians of the Diaspora Towards Baptism.
Bilingual leaflets for the Celebration of the Sacraments of Baptism, Anointing of the Sick and Marriage.
Insights into the Religious Background of the Khmers.
The First Step in Khmer for the RCIA.

The following bilingual (Cambodian/English) missals are available:
Ordinary time of the year from the second Sunday to the seventh Sunday for the years A, B, C.
Seasons of Lent for the years A,B, C.
Seasons of Advent and Christmas for the years A,B, C.
The Easter Season for the years A,B, C.
The Ordinary Time of the year A.
The Ordinary Time of the year B.
The Ordinary Time of the year C.
The Paschal Triduum.
A new edition of the Book of Songs is currently being prepared. (Cambodian)

HMONG

The following catechetical materials can be ordered/purchased from:
Rev. Daniel Taillez
Hmong Catholic Center
941 E. 5th Street
St Paul, MN 55106
(612) 771-4644

Books:
Anointing of the Sick. (Hmong and English)
Catholic Understanding of the Bible. Sr. Judy Frucci & Tom Myott (Hmong and English)
Eucharist. (Hmong and English)
Funeral Song in Hmong.
Hmong Bible, 727 pages.
Hmong/English Missalette, Prayers and the Ordinary for the Mass. (Hmong and English)
Hmong Newsletter, 3 times a year (each issue).
Holy Week. (Hmong and English)

Lord Open My Eyes, 94 pages. (Hmong)
New Hmong Songs, tape included. (Hmong and English version)
Raising Teenagers, by Deacon James Baskfield, 36 pages.
R.C.I.A., 55 pages. (Hmong and English)
Renew. (Hmong and English)
Tape About the Prayers and Songs in Hmong.
The Gospel: Our Life and Our Happiness, by Deacon Va Thai Lo.
Thirty Tapes in Hmong to Teach Hmong Catechumens, with written text, 212 pages, (Hmong); 75 page summary (English).
Vatican II: Chapter 1 and 2 of the Dogmatic Constitutions of the Church Decree on Ecumenism. (Hmong/English)
Video Tape: "The Gospel is the Light of the World," 2 hours accompanied by a booklet. (Hmong)

Hmong Cultural Patrimony Collection:
Folktales, Legends, Funeral Ritual and Marriage Songs from Anning, China.
Tales and Legends, vol. 1, 2, and 3.
The Funeral Traditional Rites, 666 pages.
Marriage Songs and Rites, vol. 1, 138 pages.
Origin of the Hmong according to Van Vinai "Confraternity," 166 pages.
First Step in Hmong; abecedaire Hmong.

LAOTIAN

The following catechetical materials can be ordered/purchased from:
Rev. Loiuis Leduc, MEP
Laotian Pastoral Center
3508 Maurice Avenue
Fort Worth, TX 76111
(817) 831-2236/4404

Books:
Anointing of the Sick.
Baptism of Adults.
Baptism of Infants.
Catechism.
Catechism According to the Creed. (English/Lao)
Gospels.
Let Us Pray. (English/Lao)
Life of Christ.
Louanges Songbook.
Marriage.
Missal for Funerals.
New Testament.
Prayers in Lao. (according to the Divine Office)
Salt of the Earth, Light of the World.

Seng Arun. (Newsletter)
Sunday Missals, Years A, B, & C.

RELIGIONS

Some Religions and Philosophies of Asian Origin

Animism

Animism is a feature of many of the basic world religions. The early peoples who inhabited the earth saw the world and nature as filled with spirits, and their experience led to the development of religions. In addition to being present in human beings, these spirits were seen as present in animals, trees, rivers, mountains, earth, celestial bodies, and the oceans and seas. The spirits could help or hinder, make one well or sick, and could communicate with humankind. The animistic understanding of life and nature is one of the most fundamental bases of humankind's religions.

Hinduism

Hinduism is perhaps the oldest and most complex religion in the world. The Hindu culture began between the second and third millenium B.C. with the arrival of the Aryan peoples into the Indus River Valley. The indigenous peoples, the Dravidians (people of southern India) practiced asceticism, yoga and private worship (puja); they also devalued the meaning of the external world. The Aryans brought with them a collection of hymns (Vedas), sacrificial rituals, numerous gods and goddesses (Devas), and the sacred language of Sanskrit. After the Aryans arrived, a fusion of the indigenous and incoming cultures occurred, thus forming the new Hinduism.

The word "Hindu" comes from the Sanskrit name for the river Indus, "Sindhu." Hinduism is probably the most tolerant of all religions, its forms ranging from simple animism to more elaborate belief systems. While "Hindu" refers to a variety of religious beliefs and practices, it generally applies to the religion of the people of India and, unlike most religions of the world, it has no identifiable founder. Although Hinduism has many followers, it has never been an aggressive missionary religion, thus it continues to be practiced mainly in India.

The basic Hindu belief is that what makes a person religious is how one lives. Anyone who lives righteously, who loves and serves others, and who works towards peace and justice in the world is considered religious.

One of the Hindu stories of creation is the myth of the cosmic person who became everything through self-sacrificial dismemberment. Another is the following Hymn of Creation which begins before the distinction of being and non-being:

Non-being then existed not nor being:
There was no air, nor sky that is beyond it.
What was concealed? Wherein? In whose protection?
And was there deep unfathomable water?

Death then existed not nor life immortal;
Of neither night nor day was any token.
By its inherent force the One breathed breathless:
No other thing than that beyond existed.
Darkness there was at first by darkness hidden;
Without distinctive marks, this all was water.
That which, becoming, by the void was covered.
That One by force of heat came into being.
Desire entered the One in the beginning:
It was the earliest seed, of thought the product.
The sages searching in their hearts with wisdom
Found out the bond of being in non-being.

(R.C. Zaehner, Translator, *Hindu Scripture*, New York: E.P. Dutton, 1966, pp. 11-12.)

Hinduism has been the source of three other religions—Buddhism, Jainism and Sikhism.

Buddhism

Buddhism began in India in the sixth century B.C. as an interpretation and outgrowth of Hinduism. By the third century B.C. it took on a missionary aspect and moved into countries such as China, Japan, Korea and Indochina.

Ultimately, Buddhism became far more popular outside of India than within India where Hinduism remained the primary religion.

Buddhism was founded by Siddhartha, a member of the Gautana clan; he has become known as Buddha, and is said to have lived from 560 to 480 B.C. It is not clear that Buddha wanted to found a new religion or even to reform Hinduism. His teachings center on self-understanding and the belief that people work out their own way of dealing with suffering and pain, rather than appealing to a God or gods for assistance.

Buddha's central teachings about humankind's challenge is presented in the following Buddhist statement about the Four Noble Truths and the Eightfold Path which leads to "Nirvana" (literally, "extinguished" or "put out like a candle").

This is the noble Eightfold Way, namely right view, right intention, right speech, right action, right livelihood, right effort, right mindfulness, right concentration. This, monks, is the Middle Path, of which the Tathagata has gained enlightenment, which produces insight and knowledge, and tends to calm, to higher knowledge, enlightenment, Nirvana.

Now this, monks, is the noble truth of pain: birth is painful, old age is painful, sickness is painful, death is painful, sorrow, lamentation, dejection, and despair are painful. Contact with unpleasant things is painful, not getting what one wishes is painful. In short the five groups of grasping are painful.

Now this, monks, is the noble truth of the cause of pain: the craving, which tends rebirth, combined with pleasure, finding pleasure here and there, namely the craving for passion, the craving for existence, the craving for nonexistence.

Now this, monks, is the noble truth of the cessation of pain, the cessation without a remainder of craving, the abandonment, forsaking, release, non-attachment.

(Pali Sermons, the first sermon. *Samyutta*, V, 420, E.J. Thomas, translator, London: Kegan, Trench, Trubner and Co., Ltd., 1935, pp. 29-33.)

Generally, Buddhists attempt to heal the pain which is inherent in humankind's struggle for existence or non-existence. The Four Noble Truths are: the universality of pain, difficulty, unsatisfactoriness (*duhkha*); its cause; its cure; and its treatment. *Duhkha* is caused by attachment, aversion and confusion; it is cured by the threefold practice of morality *(sila)*, meditation *(samadhi)*, and wisdom *(prajna)*.

As Buddhism spread into north, south, and east Asia, it developed two major lineages—Theravada Buddhism and Mahayana Buddhism.

Theravada Buddhism is the more traditional of the two major divisions, holding more closely to the original teachings of the Buddha. The major locations of Theravada Buddhism today are Sri Lanka, Burma, and the nations of Southeast Asia.

In Mahayana Buddhism, a development of Buddhism from the third century B.C., one of the most important doctrines is that every being possesses the Buddha nature and is therefore capable of becoming a Buddha. This is in contrast to the Theravada teaching that there is only one Buddha and that enlightenment is achievable by only a few.

Many Mahayana sects developed as Buddhism spread throughout the countries of Asia. Zen, for example, is a Mahayanist sect.

Taoism

Taoism can best be described as an early Chinese philosophical and religious system which views Tao (the Way) as the source and reality of humankind and nature. One of the earliest writers of Tao philosophy, and therefore considered its founder by some, was Lao-tzu who lived in the sixth century B.C. It is thought that Lao-tzu was approximately 50 years older than Confucius and that the two philosophers had conversations in which Confucius took on the role of disciple.

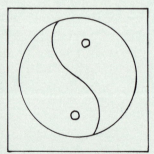

Lao-tzu was supposed to have written the Tao Te Ching (The Classic of the Way and Its Power or Virtue), a short, poetic work which has become influential in Chinese literature. In addition, Chuang-tzu who was a disciple of Lao-tzu, wrote of the practice of Taoism. The two works give some indication of the early teachings and center on the following themes:

1. The basic unity behind the universe is a mysterious and undefinable force called the Tao.

2. Life is the greatest of all possessions.

3. Life is to be lived simply.
4. Pomp and glory are to be despised.

Nothing under heaven is softer or more yielding than water; but when it attacks things hard and resistant there is not one of them that can prevail. For they can find no way of altering it. That the yielding conquers the resistant and the soft conquers the hard is a fact known by all. (From the *Tao Te Ching*)

Confucianism

Confucianism was founded by a Chinese teacher, K'ung Fu-tzu, who was born in 551 B.C. (551 B.C.-479 B.C.) Eventually, his name was latinized by western missionaries into "Confucius." Because he lived in a time of rapid social change, Confucius' goal was to establish a just social order through loving human relationships and good government. Some describe Confucianism as a system of social, political, ethical, and religious thought.

The *Analects of Confucius* contain his principal teachings which emphasize the development of the following moral virtues: humaness, goodness or love *(jen)*; filial devotion *(hsiao)*; and, propriety and courtesy *(li)*. These virtues were found in the "noble person" *(chun tzu)*, particularly in the acting out of the five relationships, namely—between parent and child, ruler and minister, husband and wife, older and younger siblings, and friend and friend.

Confucian thought was further developed by Mencius (372-289 B.C.), Hsun tzu (298-238 B.C.), and ultimately by the major Neo-Confucian teacher, Chu Hsi (1130-1200). In contrast with Buddha's tendency towards withdrawal from the world in meditative practices, Chu developed a spirituality of the times—in and for this world. It was based on a balance of religious reverence, ethical practice, scholarly investigation and political participation.

While the Buddhists saw the world and change as the source of pain and suffering, Chu Hsi and his followers welcomed change as the source of transformation in both the person and the world. Thus, Confucian spirituality involved developing one's moral nature to bring it into harmony with the larger changing cosmos.

Shinto

Shinto, the traditional religion of Japan, is practiced for the most part by Japanese, and has developed naturally—without a founder. The ancient Japanese did not have a name for their ethnic religion, however the word "Shinto" was coined in the sixth century A.D. to distinguish it from Buddhism, Taoism and Confucianism which were beginning to develop in Japan.

Shinto is a term which can be translated "the way of the

kami or gods." As a religion, Shinto embraces a broad variety of religious and national practices. Some characteristic features of Shinto are the notion of *kami* (supernatural forces or gods) which pervades all of Japanese culture, and *norito* or ritual prayers. It is a national religion, practiced for the most part by Japanese, and has developed naturally—without a founder.

The concept of *kami* is basically polytheistic, and Shinto includes prayer to the *kami*, festivals, ascetic discipline, social service, and other elements. It has touched the life of the Japanese people not so much as an organized theology or philosophy but as a code of values, a pattern of behavior and a way of thinking.

Shinto can be classified into three broad types, all of which are interrelated and not mutually exclusive: Shrine Shinto (or State Shinto), consisting of worship of the *kami* at local shrines; Sect Shinto referring to the thirteen groups formed during the nineteenth century, each with its own founder and organization; and, Domestic Shinto (or Folk Shinto), which is a simple form of Shinto which takes place in Japanese homes.

Some Suggestions for Further Reading on Religions

Anesaki, Masaharu. *History of Japanese Religion*, Rutland, VT, Tuttle, 1963.

Borelli, John. Editor. (Prepared with the members of the Faiths in the World Committee, National Association of Diocesan Ecumenical Officers).*Handbook for Interreligious Dialogue*, Morristown, NJ, Silver Burdett & Ginn, 1990.

Ching, Julia. *Confucianism and Christianity*, New York, Columbia University Press, New York,1977.

Dawson, Raymond. *Confucius*, New York, Hill and Wang, 1981.

de Bary, William T. Editor. *Sources of Indian Tradition*, New York, Columbia University Press, 1958.

de Bary, William T. Editor. *The Buddhist Tradition in India, China and Japan*, New York, Modern Library, 1969.

Earhart, H. Byron. Series editor. *Religious Traditions of the World Series*, San Francisco, Harper & Row.

   Buddhism, 1988.
   Hinduism, 1990.
   Religions of China, 1986.
   Religions of Japan, 1984.

Hinnells, John R. Editor. *A Handbook of Living Religions*. New York, Penguin Books, 1984.

Kapleau, Philip. *The Three Pillars of Zen: Teaching, Practice and Enlightenment*, Garden City, NY, Doubleday (Anchor Books), 1980.

Nielsen, Niels C., Jr. and others. *Religions of the World*, St. Martin's Press, 1983.

O'Flaherty, Wendy Doniger. *Hindu Mythology*, New York, Penguin Books, 1974.

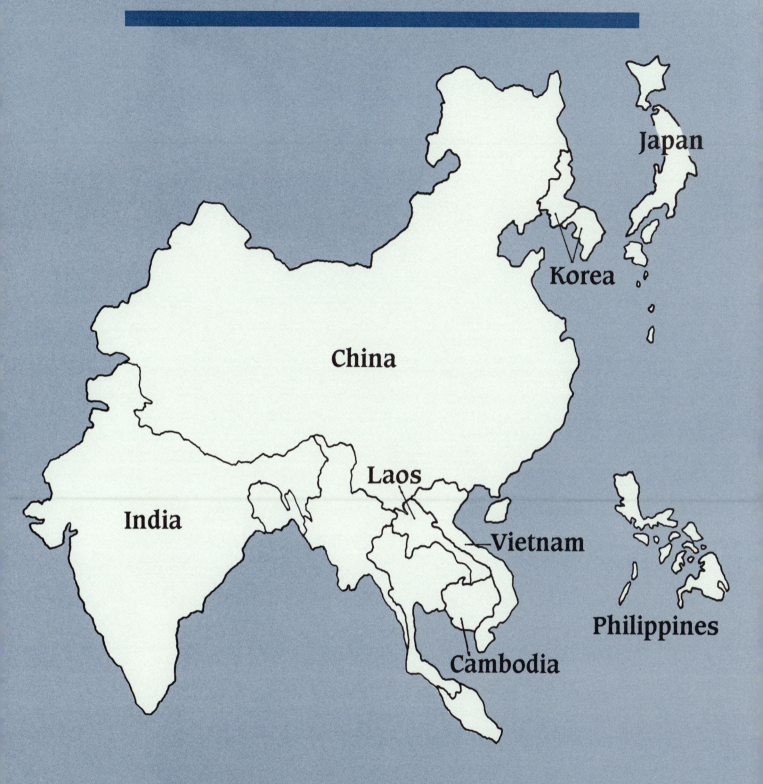